CURTSY TO THE LADY

ANNISHA
HEWITT

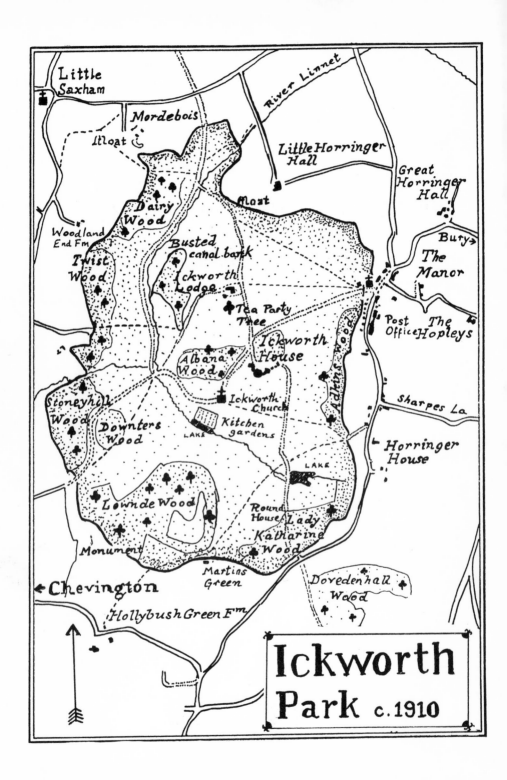

Little Saxham

Mordebois

Moat

River Linnet

Little Horringer Hall

Great Horringer Hall

Dairy Wood

Woodland End Fm

Twist Wood

Busted canal bank

Ickworth Lodge

Moat

Bury →

The Manor

Tea Party Tree

Post Office

The Hopleys

Ickworth House

Albana Wood

Adkins Wood

Stoneyhill Wood

Downters Wood

Ickworth Church

Kitchen gardens

LAKE

Sharpes La.

Horringer House

LAKE

Lownde Wood

Round House

Lady Katharine Wood

Monument

Martins Green

Dovedenhall Wood

← Chevington

Hollybush Green Fm

Ickworth Park c. 1910

CURTSY TO THE LADY

A Horringer childhood

by

ZOË WARD

TERENCE DALTON LIMITED
LAVENHAM . SUFFOLK
1985

Published by
TERENCE DALTON LIMITED

ISBN 0 86138 041 X

Text photoset in 10/11pt Century Schoolbook

Printed in Great Britain at The Lavenham Press Limited,
Lavenham, Suffolk

Contents

To Mrs Lainson,
with many thanks for her help,
and to those who were born
and bred in Horringer

Foreword

by Mrs M.M.E. Lainson

Mrs Ward was born in the first decade of the century, in the village of Horringer, in the county of West Suffolk and, apart from a short period doing her teacher-training in the twenties, she has lived there ever since. Her father was the Postmaster for many years. When she married, she left her paternal home at the village post office, crossed what is now the A143 road and took up her residence in a beautiful cottage on the other side of the village green, a full thirty-eight yards away! The great gates of Ickworth Park are immediately to her left; the church stands diagonally across most of her daily progressions; the school, where she taught for many years as headmistress, meant a walk of nearly a hundred yards from house to work. The circle of houses around the green and along the Street bounded her childhood, contained her friends and later her pupils, but never confined her interests, her vision or her enthusiasm.

After her retirement she set about recording the history of the Hervey family of Ickworth, whose influence in the village was paramount until the end of the First World War, as her childhood story tells. She went on to write a history of Horringer, the proceeds from which she donated equally to the building of a new community centre and the new cricket pavilion.

Thus throughout her life she has served the village of Horringer in numerous capacities. She has been chairman of the Parish Council and continues to be an active member of it, under the present chairmanship of her son. She has been involved in the building of the new community centre from its inception and now controls its busy diary. She did not like the great influx of people in the 60's and 70's, but she controls her dismay and has many friends among the newcomers.

Altogether her life, bounded within the parish of Horringer and Ickworth, at the same time circles the quiet revolution that has taken place throughout the English countryside this century, without disturbing the deep roots and traditions of our society.

Horringer House,
Horringer

CHAPTER ONE

A Feudal Village

WILLIAM WHITE'S *History, Gazetteer & Directory of Suffolk* published in 1855 contains a concise yet revealing entry concerning the village of Horringer:

> Horningsheath, commonly called Horringer, is a neat and pleasant village, two miles West-South-West of Bury St Edmunds, on the east side of the extensive and pleasant park of Ickworth. The village also includes the hamlet of Horsecroft.

From the old name Horningsherth we get an idea who was the first owner of the village. He was probably an Anglo-Saxon or even a Viking named Horn, who at some time between A.D. 500 and 900 settled in the village and gave his name to the place. Ing meant "the family of" and herth meant the "estate or settlement", so Horningsherth indicates the settlement of the Horn family.

The first owner of Horringer was Theodred, at one time Bishop of East Anglia and later Bishop of London. In his will dated A.D. 959 he left "the land at . . . Horninggesherthe and at Ickworthe . . . to St Edmund's Church" by which he meant the Abbey in Bury St Edmunds. For the next six hundred years the Abbey held the village, or manor, of Horringer.

After the Dissolution the manor was sold to various people, including Sir Thomas Darcy, afterwards Lord Darcy of Chich. He sold it to Sir Robert Southwell, Master of the Rolls, and his grandson sold it in 1583 to Sir Robert Jermyn of Rushbrooke, so Horringer became part of the Rushbrooke estate, the Jermyns owning it for a hundred and twenty years. When the last male Jermyn died the estate passed to Mary, the eldest daughter of the last Lord Jermyn, who was married to Sir Robert Davers. The marriage of Elizabeth, daughter of Sir Jermyn Davers, to Frederick, fourth Earl of Bristol and Bishop of Derry, brought Horringer into the Hervey family in 1806.

The village still has a very neat and attractive appearance, partly due to the fact that many of the houses stand well back from the road, and there are some very fine trees on the green and in the street. Another attractive feature is that Adkin's Wood, planted about 1800, which runs for the length of the village behind the cottages on the west of the street, forms a perfect background for the thatched cottages with their walls of lath and plaster.

1

Horringer was a typical "estate" village, and up to the First World War the residents, among whom I count myself, could see no reason why it should not remain "the same yesterday, today and for ever." However, like countless other villages in the country, Horringer has felt the wind of change blowing through it, rising to gale force during the last twenty years. When the first whisperings of development came we brushed them aside as being just another scare, until the builders moved in! That was the end of an era.

Until then Horringer had been a quiet semi-feudal village with the great advantage of having Ickworth Park on its doorstep, with the Hervey family influencing every aspect of village life. It is difficult for incomers to realise how much good the Herveys did and how greatly the family was respected by the natives of Horringer.

When I was a child, Lord Bristol, the fourth Marquis, Lady Bristol and their two daughters, Lady Marjorie and Lady Phyllis, lived at Ickworth. Lord Bristol was an ex-navy man, having served in that branch of the armed forces until he succeeded his uncle, the third Marquis, in 1907. He was not often seen in the village, preferring to spend his time in the park, spudding thistles. Now and again we saw him cycling down to Bury on his fixed-wheel bicycle, going to the Shire Hall on council business.* We children regarded him as someone outside our orbit, someone who lived at the mansion and owned the park and all the houses in the village and for miles around. There were many stories about his strong language, but that was put down to the fact that he had been a sailor. Tall and very good looking, he had simple tastes and disliked functions and having to be formal.

He was against progress and modernisation. To every request involving any change, he had a stock answer "What was good enough for your grandfather should be good enough for you." There was no telephone at Ickworth until about 1936; Lord Bristol hated the machine and said it didn't give you time to think of a reason for saying "no!"

Lady Bristol, quiet and homely and extremely wealthy, was in temperament the opposite to her husband. She was very fond of animals and was usually accompanied in her walks across the park by two small black dogs, schupperkes, Rosie and Bessie, or names like that. Those dogs were hated by Lord Bristol and the male staff because they had the horrible habit of hiding under the settee or armchair and nipping the ankles of any unsuspecting visitor. The footmen watched their opportunity and when Lady

---

*Lord Bristol was chairman of West Suffolk County Council for more than twenty years. He was made an honorary freeman of Bury St Edmunds in 1943 for his "eminent and valuable" services to the borough.

Bristol was not looking they would help Rosie or Bessie on their way with a swift, well-judged kick. The story was told of the day when Lord Bristol was "treed" by the two black fiends; although his bellows for help, together with his naval description of all dogs, might have been heard in Bury, up the tree he had to stay until Lady Bristol could be found and brought to the scene to call off the dogs.

Their two daughters were well known in the village. Although their mother was one of the wealthiest ladies in the country, they were brought up in almost Spartan simplicity, never being allowed jam and cake for tea—just one or the other. They had a

The Rotunda at Ickworth, begun by the Fourth Earl of Bristol, Bishop of Derry, in 1795. It was still incomplete when the Earl-Bishop died in Italy eight years later.

governess, of course, who was far more regal than the marchioness herself; Miss Henrietta Swete was large and stately, ruling her charges with a rod of iron. I think she left round about 1916. There were other governesses, of course, for French, German and Art. Both girls were very good at art, as was their mother.

Apart from Lord and Lady Bristol and their two daughters, there were always other members of the family staying there. The two I can remember quite clearly were Lady Geraldine, widow of the third marquis, and her sister-in-law, Lady Mary Hervey. They were usually driven over to the village in one of the carriages drawn by two horses, with a coachman and a groom in attendance. They always wore black cloaks, dresses and bonnets, but apart from the similarity in the colour of their clothes, they were very different in appearance. The Dowager Marchioness, Lady Geraldine, was small and dainty and still very pretty. She looked extravagant—and was. She was knocked down and killed by a car at Hyde Park Corner in 1920, when she was eighty. Lady Mary was tall and rather masculine looking, twice the size of Lady Geraldine, and rather domineering. She was a beautiful needle-woman. She died in 1928, and after that I do not think the carriages were ever used again.

There was a large staff of servants, although the Bristols lived very quietly, apart from shooting parties in the season. The most important indoor servant was the butler, or house steward, to use the old name. Mr William Collins was the butler during our childhood, and after. He was not at all like a typical butler, being small and not at all pompous. He was very quietly spoken, but very efficient. I do not think there was an under-butler, but there were always two stalwart footmen, each over six feet tall and broad in proportion. They did not have powdered hair when I knew them, but until 1907 they had been obliged to powder their hair. They wore pin-striped black trousers, crimson waistcoats and dark green doeskin jackets, ornamented with silver buttons, each with the Hervey crest on it. As far as I can remember, they wore ordinary white shirts and black ties. In contrast to all this splendour, Mr Collins was dressed in a sober black jacket, or sometimes a frock coat.

There were under-footmen, odd-job men, lamp men, bootboys, men to chop kindling and lay fires, to fill scuttles and do another hundred and one jobs.

Most important and imposing of the female staff was the housekeeper, Mrs Paris, of whom Mr Collins was scared stiff, or so it was said in the village. She was so regal, she could have passed for the marchioness any day. She always wore black, a satin blouse and thicker skirt, with a belt carrying a chatelaine at her waist. Her white hair was piled on the top of her head and she wore rimless pince-nez. She kept the staff, male and female, on a very tight rein, and she was such a contrast to Mr Collins; she would have made three of him, anyway. Next in importance was Miss Sangster, the cook, who was not as imposing as Mrs Paris, yet was just as efficient. She was quieter, but not at all downtrodden by the housekeeper; after all, she was less able to be spared than Mrs Paris!

Then there were four parlourmaids, half a dozen kitchen maids and the same number of scullery maids, otherwise known as tweenies, who were the lowest form of life. Extra help was called in from the village when any large party was held. Upstairs were the ladies' maids. Miss Jones, a tiny Welshwoman, was Lady Bristol's personal maid, the girls had a maid between them, and Lord Bristol had his valet. There were extra maids for visitors, and of course, Miss Swete had her maid. When the girls were small there was a nurse, an under nurse, a night nurse, and nursery maids. Later there were schoolroom maids, though they took the place of nursery maids.

The outdoor staff was just as large. First there were the heads of departments. Mr Henry Coster was head gardener, and he had a staff of a dozen or more; Mr John Curtis was head forester,* and he had a staff of at least a dozen; Mr Kitcatte was head coachman, and eight or nine men worked in the stables; later there was Mr Harry Noyes, the chauffeur, and he had an under-chauffeur; there were carpenters and painters, who worked in the house itself; there was an electrician when electricity was installed; there was Mr Herod, the head gamekeeper, and he had at least six under-keepers and the same number of warreners. Then there was an army of men employed in the pleasure grounds; there was the dairy, where the milk was made into butter, the milk that was not needed for the house being sold to the village people; there were the cowmen, and the shepherds. There were also many men who "worked in the park" but I don't know what they did—Billy Parker caught moles, I know that.

Then a lot of outside people were employed—everyone in the village worked on the estate. The men worked on the farms, or in the park, and the women worked as indoor servants or as laundresses. The blacksmiths shoed the ponies and horses; many women in the village did the washing; odd alterations to clothes were done by dressmakers in the village; some women plucked the chickens and pheasants when there was a big party.

We were regularly reminded of the Family in other ways, too. When they were in residence, which was the greater part of the year, we used to hear two bells in the evening. One was rung at

*Mr Curtis came as head forester in 1900 and did not retire until 1951, when he was eighty.

twenty to eight, and that was the "dressing bell;" the second bell was rung at eight o'clock, and that was the "dinner bell." The practice of ringing these bells was discontinued at the outbreak of the Second World War, but when we were children those two bells ruled our summer evenings—"You can stay out till the dinner bell goes." It was very easy not to hear the bells!

The bells were never rung if Lord and Lady Bristol were away, but they were not away very often—just six weeks in March and April for "The Season" and a few odd weekends. Lord and Lady Bristol did not like going away, although they kept a house in London, at 6 St James's Square, but their absence from Ickworth enabled the house to be thoroughly spring-cleaned.

The Bristols were not great ones for entertaining, although they had several shooting parties during the winter. For those parties the house was full, and even the rooms in the Rotunda were used. It was always said in the village that when the dining room in the Rotunda was in use the footmen used to cycle along the corridors underground so that the food on their trays should not get too cold. On the occasion of these parties the bedrooms in

Table silver like this provided quite a cleaning job for the servants at Ickworth.

the Rotunda were also used; cans of hot water had to be carried up even to the topmost bedrooms by the housemaids every morning and evening, and when baths were required it meant more journeys up those stairs. Of course coal had to be carried up as well, as fires were lit in every bedroom, shooting parties being held in the winter when the Rotunda was at its chilliest. The servants certainly earned their five shillings (25p) a week in those days, yet it was the ambition of most of the village girls and boys to go into service at Ickworth.

Although Lord and Lady Bristol were too remote to come into contact with many of the village people they, especially Lady Bristol, always seemed to know exactly what was going on, which was very mystifying to the local people. Although they were greatly respected, and certainly not personally feared, they were like gods on Olympus—remote from the daily round. It was a very brave person who dared to consult them or to complain to them.

Cottages were constantly needing repair and needless to say were never modernised. Funnily enough, no opprobrium for this reflected on Lord Bristol, but only on his agents who, I must say, were more than able to look after themselves. While Lord Bristol was held in respectful awe, his agents were feared and disliked. "Anyone would think that it was their own money they were spending," people used to say when complaining that it seemed impossible to get them to do even the most necessary repairs.

Lord Bristol probably had no idea of this. In extremity, some bold person would approach Lady Bristol; the requested repair would be carried out, but it was advisable to avoid the estate agent for ever after. So all the contacts, complaints and consultations had to be made with the person who was most feared, and disliked, in the village, the estate agent. He had great power over all the estate tenants, and much went on in the name of the Bristols that the Bristols knew nothing about.

The first agent I can remember, and that only dimly, was Mr Donne. He did not live in Horringer, but in Bury, and he rode out every day on his big grey horse. Many a boy, up to no good, was chased by Mr Donne. He was followed by Mr Moir, who lived at Little Horringer Hall and had an office in Bury. Slim and dapper, he was a very good cricketer. He and Mr Donne were, for agents, quite well liked and respected. Their successor, who had been a clerk in the estate office, was often harsh and inconsiderate, especially to those who knew he held their job and house in his hands. People would let water come through the roof on to the bed rather than complain to him.

The only time I can remember hearing of interference from Lord and Lady Bristol in village affairs was when the idea of having a fair at the Flower Show was suggested; they objected to that, and so for some years the idea was shelved, but later on they withdrew their objections—and the fair came.

There had been very little building done in the village over the years. Almost the last houses to be built were the pair now called Lady Bristol's Cottages, built in 1907. Another pair of cottages, still unnamed, were built down Westley Lane about 1912; they were "tied" to Great Horringer Hall Farm. Four more were built a few years later in Little Horringer in what is called Slough Lane; but it was to be forty years before any more building was carried out.

There were some changes, of course, like the moving of the forge, but they were few and far between. The old forge was between the maple tree and the church hedge, right in the middle of the green, and by the middle of the nineteenth century it was a very tumbledown affair. The blacksmith at that time was Benjamin Pryke, known to everyone as "Doc", possibly because in the old days blacksmiths acted as dentists as well as farriers. There had been Prykes in Horringer from 1563 and in Ickworth from 1629, nearly all of them blacksmiths. "Doc" had in the early part of his life lived in Ickworth, at Mordebois, but when the forge there closed about 1814 he moved to Horringer, into the old dilapidated forge in the middle of the green.

When a new forge and house were built about 1850 "Doc" flatly refused to move from his old house. A fierce old man, he had a habit when annoyed of walking about the green brandishing a

sword which he said he had used at the Battle of Waterloo, and against such a weapon arguments proved useless. "Doc" would not listen to reason, he was staying where he was.

At last a plan was made, however. On market day some of his friends took "Doc" to Bury and got him dead drunk. While they were away others pulled down the old house and forge and moved all "Doc's" belongings over to the new house. "Doc" was at the end of the day brought back and deposited in his new abode. When eventually he came to, there he was, and there was nothing he could do about it. Of what he said there is no record!

In a dry summer the marks of the foundations of the old forge can still be seen on the green.

Traffic was negligible—I mean motor traffic, of course. There were about four cars in the village up to the 1914-18 war. Mr Charters, of Horringer Manor, went in for Rolls Royces; he had a bright yellow one first, and later a dark green one, with large brass headlamps. Mr Tollemache of Hopleys had a small open four-seater, the Bristols had a Daimler and the Bevans of Ickworth Lodge had a small black car.

There were no motor lorries or vans, no buses, no juggernauts. The traffic consisted mainly of farm carts and tumbrils, with pony traps used for social occasions. Carriages were dying out, though I can just remember seeing one from Ickworth House being driven through Horringer occasionally, usually when some of the older members of the family came to stay.

The new forge to which "Doc" Pryke was forcibly removed about 1850, as it is today and as it was when there were horses to be shod and carts and waggons to be repaired and harrows to be made.

There were very few bicycles up to 1914, and what a status symbol they were! Never mind how old and rusty it might be, possessing a bike was like owning a diamond tiara. The children of the "gentry" had their bicycles, but the rest of us relied on our pony—Shanks's pony.

There were a couple of traps that could be hired. Mr Horne at the *Six Bells* had one which could take six, including the driver. His mare was called Daisy and was a horrid liver and white colour. Mr Rolfe, who lived in College House for a time, had a pony cart for hire. His pony was pure white, and rejoiced in the name of Kitty-Sooty. This pony had one peculiarity: it would always stop at the *Spread Eagle* on the way home from Bury and would not budge until it had been given half a pint of beer.

People have been known to walk to Bury and back three times a day, about eighteen miles in all, especially in a case of illness. First there was the walk in to get the doctor, then in again for the medicine, then later in the day there might be something else the invalid wanted, so back they would go again. In those days people considered that legs were there to be used, and were not just for ornament.

Now and again a "poor" person would be given a lift into Bury in one of the high gigs used by the gentry. But this was a mixed blessing, as they were told to be careful of this and not to touch that; many preferred to walk.

Getting a lift into Bury on market day with a farmer was all right, but it was not so easy to get a lift for the homeward journey. Many of the farmers took a drop too much, and either they went to sleep and let the old horse get home as best it could, or else they whipped it up until it went along "as though the devil hisself was arter it."

One very popular way of getting into market was by carrier's cart; the fare was fourpence return for an adult, twopence for a child. There were two carriers who came through Horringer twice a week, on Wednesdays and Saturdays, on their way from Wickhambrook to Bury. Their carts were like great open hay wains, with seats for six or eight people along each side and room for two or three along each short side; children, parcels, and sometimes a lamb or a piglet would be put on the floor in the middle. The carriers died out with the First World War and the coming of the buses.

The carts used to go through Horringer about half past ten in the morning, which means they must have left Wickhambrook about half past eight, as they did not go much quicker than a walking pace. The long-distance passengers must have been frozen long before they got to Bury. The carts were usually full before they reached Horringer, so those people picked up in the village had to squeeze in as best they could and travelled in the greatest discomfort. Funnily enough, the same applies to the present-day buses—it is always the Horringer people who are left behind.

The best-remembered of the carriers were Mr Charles Cooke, who had a smart, clean, shining cart and was in great demand, and old Jon'than Harris, from Chedburgh, who was much less popular; there was usually room in his cart for Horringer people. Jon'than was the dirtiest old man I have ever seen; he used to wear the filthiest coat you could imagine, and an old squashed-up felt hat. And his cart was like him; it was never even cleaned, let alone polished. Jon'than's eyes were grey and bleary, topped by thick bushy eyebrows that stuck out beyond the brim of his hat. Everyone who knew Jon'than remembers his beard, short and tufty, grey and stained from the old black pipe he used to smoke. He never carried a handkerchief, and he smelt of snuff—or perhaps it was just the smell of dirt. Old Jon'than never had a word to say; people who rode with him regularly for years cannot remember ever hearing him speak.

His horse was old and knock-kneed and did not seem to know how to put one foot in front of the other. It always looked as though it would never reach Bury, to say nothing about ever getting home again, yet time after time it did get to Bury, taking an hour to cover the three miles from Horringer. Jon'than used to put up at the *Half Moon* public house, which stood in the Butter Market where the *Playhouse* stood later. He used to leave there at four o'clock sharp, winter and summer, and he cannot have arrived at Wickhambrook till about half past eight—a long day.

It was no joke climbing into any carrier's cart, especially in those days of long skirts. Imagine trying to get in with a couple of heavy baskets and a long skirt! Either you dropped your baskets or you trod on your skirt. You had to get your foot on an iron step fixed near the off-front wheel, then you heaved and clambered up, usually falling in head first. Or else, if you were agile enough, you stood on the hub of the wheel, and climbed over the side.

A polite driver would have helped his passengers in, but not Jon'than. He would sit, staring straight in front of him, apparently unconcerned whether you broke your neck or merely a couple of limbs. All the same, it was better than walking.

There were ways and means by which the carrier knew if you wanted to travel in his cart. In fine weather the prospective passengers waited at their gates for him; in winter they either stuck a piece of paper in a front window or put a kind of flag in their garden, and the carrier would stop for them. It was a saying in Horringer at one time, "I went in Harris, and I came back in Harris."

CHAPTER TWO

The Weekly Routine

SINCE MOST of the village men worked on the Bristol Estate or on one of the farms the procession of men drifting into the park before breakfast was an everyday sight. "Drifting" is the operative word; that is all some of them ever did. Wages were small but jobs were secure, and even when old age pensions were introduced the older men still walked into the park every morning to sweep up a few leaves, stub up a few thistles or just sit on the handle of a barrow until it was time to go home at six o'clock. There was no five-day week until after the First World War and everyone worked the full six days, though I think work finished an hour earlier on Saturdays. There was no need for the men to go to Bury; their wives did all the shopping during the week, and the men could have their hair cut by an amateur in the village.

The women had their own routine of work. On Monday the women washed—or to put it in another way they did the week's washing. Horringer was known as "Bury's wash-tub" as so many village women took in washing, which was delivered to them on Saturday afternoon by pony or donkey-cart. There was also washing to be done for the big houses. Ickworth had its own laundry, but much of the linen was sent out to women in the village, packed in large wicker baskets. It took a whole day to iron one of the large linen tablecloths, or so I am told.

Every house had its own copper, the fire for which was laid on Sundays by the man of the house, if you were lucky! He also filled the copper with soft water from the water butts, again if you were lucky. Many women filled the coppers themselves and struggled to get their fires alight by the crack of dawn on Mondays. There was plenty of room in the gardens for linen lines to hold the newly washed clothes, but, knowing our weather, many houses must have had washing hanging about most of the week. As can be imagined, the Monday wash was a Herculean operation, as the actual clothes washed were of heavy material.

Tuesdays or Thursdays, again depending on the weather, were ironing days. On Wednesdays many of the women, those who

Washing linen in a galvanised "tin" wash-tub; Horringer used to be known as "Bury's Wash-tub" because so many women in the village took in washing.

13

didn't go by carrier, walked to Bury and toiled home with laden shopping baskets, pausing to rest at the "Thank God" tree; the Bench Oak half-way along the road between Horringer and Bury and still there in 1985, with a new seat surrounding it. On Fridays, with the washing and shopping done for the week, the only worry was hanging on until the men came home with their wages on Saturday. It was a sort of lull before starting the round all over again.

On Saturdays the dirty linen was brought from the big houses and the clean linen collected and taken away. Sometimes on Saturday afternoons the week's baking would be done, as there was not a great deal of time for this on Sunday morning. In many cases, however, the baking was left till Sunday morning rather than heating up the oven twice, thus using twice the amount of fuel—all these things had to be considered.

Saturday night was bath night. As this was the era of large families and no one, except in the large houses, had a bathroom, having a bath was an operation of some magnitude. Soon after midday on Saturday the copper was filled and the fire lighted. The water would be heating all the afternoon and after tea the fun began. The tin bath was dragged in from outside and put in front of the kitchen fire. Water was put in from the copper, and the youngest (or the two youngest or even the three youngest) children were put in the bath while the rest of the family carried on with their normal occupations. The first instalment finished in the bath, they were given their suppers, if any, and sent to bed. More water was added, the next in age was bathed, and so on. By the time the last member of the family took the plunge, the water was more like mud and, although more hot water had been added from time to time, it was barely warm. Those were the days!

On Sunday, of course, everyone went to church; most people went twice a day. Men who did not go to church were liable to face the sack when they turned up for work on Monday morning. Puddings were always put on to boil before going to church; a long-winded parson was known as a "Pudden Spoiler". After the midday meal, when the washing-up was finished, parents and children went for a walk in the park, returning home in time for tea and evensong.

Looking back, it seems really strange that the First World War brought about such a radical change in the clothes people wore. Before it, everyone was bundled up in layers of clothing; they probably wore so much because they could not afford unlimited fuel to heat their draughty rooms, and their thick clothes did keep them fairly warm.

As I remember, in winter the women wore long full skirts of some thick material; serge was popular as it wore well. These skirts were usually of some dull colour, black, brown, navy or dark green, and were decorated with rows of braid for trimming. Blouses worn with these skirts varied according to the wealth of the wearer; silk blouses with high necks and ornamented with rows and rows of narrow lace or tiny tucks were very popular with those who could afford them, but the more usual wear was cotton blouses for summer and flannel ones for winter. These were of no special colour.

Costumes were the favourite outdoor wear, with long thick overcoats for winter. All wore lace up or button boots, usually black, with black or brown stockings, hand knitted. Brown boots and brown stockings were a status symbol.

Cardigans were beginning to replace shawls, except for the very old, who still preferred shawls. Old ladies still wore their caps, and very smart they looked in these frilly lace beribboned concoctions, but they were on the way out.

An advertisement for "baths of every description" supplied by a Suffolk ironmongers.

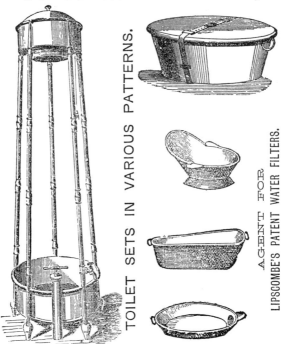

Innumerable petticoats were worn, usually a flannelette one, then two or more cotton or calico ones, the top one being more decorative, with hand-made lace or embroidery at the bottom. These petticoats were hand made, and the ones made of finer material such as cotton or lawn were elaborately embroidered, with tiny tucks and drawn thread work, smocking or broderie anglaise. How the women could do such fine work by dim lamp light or even candles, I can't imagine.

Corsets or "stays" were worn under the petticoats. These were more like suits of armour, and were so tightly laced that it was impossible to bend or move freely. Under the corsets a cotton or

The women wore large hats; Mrs Cooke, headmistress of the Infants' School, was no exception.

calico "shift" or chemise was worn. These "shifts" were also hand made, elaborately tucked, and adorned with crocheted lace. Ribbon was not often used on these undergarments, as it had to be bought; sometimes bebé, or very narrow ribbon, was threaded through some of the more special garments, but for the ordinary housewife garments which were not seen tended to be plain, except for decorations like tucks, which cost nothing extra.

"Drawers" or bloomers were of calico, and were plain. There was a gathered waistband, and the ends of the legs were gathered into bands, the waistband and leg bands being fastened by buttons. In winter, flannelette drawers were worn.

Very often a bodice was worn above the stays. This was a larger edition of the modern "bra".

Nightdresses were of calico in the summer and flannel or flannelette in the winter, decorated with tucks or crocheted lace. Sometimes the bodice part was smocked and the sleeves were smocked at the wrists. A favourite decoration on the winter nightdresses was herring-bone stitching. These garments were voluminous; considering the poverty of the ordinary people, I should have thought much material could have been saved if they had been cut on narrower lines. Shifts were kept on under nightdresses.

The men's clothes were just as thick and cumbersome as the women's. Men wore heavy woollen or flannel vests next to the skin, long woollen combinations, and thick flannel shirts in winter and cotton ones in summer. The shirts were home made, with detachable collars, but working men rarely wore collars or ties on weekdays. There was always a neckband with studs, one at the back and one at the front; open-necked shirts were never seen. Working trousers were usually of brown corduroy, tied at the ankles and beneath the knees with string or straps. Braces, not belts, kept up the trousers.

For the working man, boots were the only footwear until after the 1914–18 war. Thick woollen socks were worn under the boots. I don't remember ever seeing Wellingtons.

Everyone, men, women and children, wore hats; in fact, no one ever went out bareheaded. The women wore large hats of straw, felt or velour, lavishly decorated with artificial fruit or flowers, feathers and ribbons. The men wore cloth caps for work and bowlers for "best". Sometimes in the summer both men and women wore straw hats or "boaters" as they were called. When I was old enough to go to the County School in Bury the girls wore "boaters" in summer, but for some reason they were called "straw bargees".

Babies wore woollen bonnets, and small girls wore woollen caps or hats which were plainer editions of their mothers' headgear. Boys wore caps—not the schoolboy type, but flat caps like their fathers. Only gypsies wore head scarves.

The hats were kept on by hatpins, usually two per hat. The children's hats were kept on by elastic under the chin, and the boys' caps were kept on by faith. They were usually too large anyway, and came down almost to the eyebrows.

The children wore clothes which were smaller replicas of the clothes worn by their parents. Many girls wore stiffly starched white pinafores over their dresses for school, these being exchanged for limp coloured cotton ones when they returned home. They did not wear such large "stays" as their elders but they all wore some kind of stiff garment round their middles.

These "fashions" were changing quickly. Pinafores were almost "out" by the time I went to school, and we wore garnments called Liberty bodices instead of stays. Hair slides were beginning to replace hair ribbons, and knitted stockings, especially black ones, were becoming unfashionable. Boots were no longer worn by the girls, and only one petticoat instead of three or four.

The boys wore Norfolk jackets and stiff white collars for school. Their shirts were not changed very often—trousers reached the knee, where they met long woollen stockings which came up to meet them. Boots, with hobnails, or blakeys, and in some cases heel irons, were worn. There were no sports clothes, the boys just took off their jackets to play their games, even cricket, which was far more popular than football, being played in boots. The buying of a new pair of boots was an event of tremendous importance.

Everyone had a different set of clothes for "best" or Sunday wear. After two or more years' wear as "best", the length of time

Percy Curtis, son of the head-master of the "Big School", wear-ing the Norfolk jacket and stiff white collar which was almost uniform wear for the older boys.

depending on home circumstances, a new outfit was bought and the "best" became "second-best"; clothes were not usually taken straight in for everyday wear.

The chief source of clothes was the jumble sales, which were held two or three times a year. With all the large houses in the village being occupied, usually by families with children, there was plenty of jumble. Sixty years ago jumble sales were godsends to many people on small incomes, and the sale was more like a pitched battle with no holds barred than a genteel sale raising money for church funds.

No one altered any garment bought at a jumble sale, so that Mrs Smith would wear a dress of Lady X's just as Lady X had worn it, trimmings and all; very suitable for doing the week's washing in, I must say.

Looking back on the first two decades of the century, it seems to me that a major factor in everyone's life then was the incidence or threat of illness or disease. It is true that things were getting better, with more attention being paid to cleanliness, suitable food

18

and healthier surroundings, yet we were only just out of the era when seven children and their mother had died one after the other from tuberculosis; the story in the village was that as soon as one child died, the next one showing symptoms of "consumption" was put into the bed vacated by the one who had died—but I don't think I believe that. This unhappy family lived in one of the Yew Tree Cottages.

There were still cases of TB in the village when I was a girl. Ivy Boreham, whose parents lived in Manor Lane and who was in our class at school, suffered from this dread illness. To our eyes she had a lovely healthy complexion—but the bright flush on her cheeks was a symptom of the disease, had we children but known. She had every attention, good food, plenty of milk, and one of those outdoor huts in which she slept, but she was often away from school with a cold or a cough. We were sent to visit her every weekend until she died in July, 1923. Five years later her father, Mr James Boreham, died of the same disease at the age of forty-seven even though, being a gardener at Hopleys, he had spent most of his time in the open air. Those two were the last people to die of TB in Horringer.

With the changing times the expectation of life increased to a quite surprising extent. There were eight burials in Horringer in 1882, four of them being of children under a year old and three of them of people under forty; the odd one out had reached the age of sixty-eight. Forty years later, in 1922, the number of burials was the same, but the oldest person buried had reached the ripe old age of eighty-eight and the youngest was forty-seven; not a single child had died. Another forty years on, in 1962, the average age of those retiring to the churchyard was seventy-two.

By the Twenties those children who did die young died as a result of accidents. The first accident involving a car occurred in April, 1921, when Joan Savage, the eleven-year-old daughter of the headmistress at the infants' school, was killed at Sharpe's Lane corner when her bicycle was in collision with a car. There were occasional accidents on the farms, too; Harry Pask was gored to death by a bull, and a worker at Great Horringer Hall farm was crushed to death by a laden tumbril which ran backwards. One or two people dropped down dead, and one or two committed suicide, but for the most part people were living a lot longer.

The age of injections for everything had not yet begun, however, and there were periodic outbreaks of measles, whooping cough, mumps, chickenpox and scarlet fever. Smallpox was dying out, thanks largely to vaccination, which was compulsory unless a child's parents objected on medical or religious grounds. Isolation of children suffering from infectious diseases was supposed to be strictly enforced but it rarely was; those children who had been

19

excluded from school because their ailment was "catching" mixed with those not yet affected as soon as school was over. In those days of large families the exclusion of "contacts" sometimes meant that children would be away from school for weeks on end as one member of the family after another became ill.

Dirty heads were becoming the exception rather than the rule. I have been told that at one time, in the late nineteenth century, the headmaster of Horringer school was an expert at squashing lice with his ruler when he saw the insects walking on the desks as he went round looking at the children's work. The regular visits of the "nit-nurse", and the shame of children having to take a note home, made the mothers more anxious that their children's heads should be clean.

More attention was being paid to teeth, too. Regular visits from the school dentist were a great help in educating children to look after their teeth, though few children visited their own dentist regularly. They suffered until the school dentist came round again; oil of cloves was supposed to give the most relief to a toothache sufferer.

Colds and coughs were common in winter, and many of the older people suffered from "the bronchitis" as soon as the cold weather set in. A cure for chestiness was a tallow plaster on the chest; this was a piece of brown paper, liberally sprinkled with grease drops from a tallow candle, or as an alternative, drops of goose grease. Sore throats were eased by tying a stocking round the throat when you went to bed; quite sensible, as the stockings were thick woollen ones. Another remedy was blackcurrant tea, made by pouring boiling water on to a tablespoon of blackcurrant jam, home made of course; when the liquid had cooled, it was slipped slowly, not swallowed at a gulp.

A common ailment in the winter was chilblains. Luckily I've never had a chilblain in my life, but I can remember children coming to school with their feet and hands bound up, and suffering tortures all day. It was said the pain and irritation would be eased if the affected areas were rubbed with snow.

In those days there was not enough money coming in to buy ointments, or to pay the doctor's bills. There was some system whereby, if you were very poor (and who wasn't in those days) you could go on the "panel"; some doctors would give free treatment to patients who paid a small but regular sum into the scheme—this was long before the National Health Service, of course. That was considered an arrangement for the very poor and rather despised by the rest of the community, many of whom died rather than go to a "panel" doctor. Many of those who called in a "private" doctor never paid their bills, and never intended to—but at least they weren't "panel" patients!

A pony and trap such as the doctor used when visiting his patients.

In those days doctors came out to visit their patients; there was no question of making an appointment at the surgery a day or two in advance. A member of the family would take a message to the doctor's surgery or house and the doctor would come out, either in a trap or on his bicycle, or in his car—not many doctors had cars before 1914. There was much more illness about in those days, but doctors were not so busy as they are now because they were not called unless it was absolutely necessary, because there was the doctor's bill to pay.

There seem to have been many more handicapped people around when I was young; I think many of them could have been cured had they been born ten or twenty years later. The one I remember best was Holy Joe; I do not know his real name, but he gained his nickname from his habit of quoting from the Bible at great length. Often to be seen walking up and down the road between Horringer and Bury, as often as not pushing a barrow, he was harmless enough if rather frightening to small children. His favourite haunt was under the bridge just before the Bench Oak (on the Horringer side of the tree), from which he would suddenly rise up in front of you and frighten you to death. Nobody took any notice of him, though, he just wandered up and down the road in his dirty, shapeless old mac; he was a part of the landscape.

Two villagers were deformed. One was a hunchback who always wore red socks; and his sister was somewhat eccentric— we youngsters used to think she had a moustache and beard.

21

The shoemaker, Mr Barkham, who lived up Sharpe's Lane, had only one leg; a local farmer had only one arm. And my Aunt Tot, who lived next door to us, had contracted polio when she was two years old and never walked again without using crutches; she used to get about on her knees. My aunt—her name was Caroline Edwards, but I called her Aunt Tot—always said she had been born too soon, because if she had been born later she could have been cured. In spite of her disabilities she lived to within a month of her ninetieth birthday.

These were afflictions we could see, but there were people suffering from less visible handicaps; to look at them we did not always realise people were suffering from things we called "diabetrice" or "various veins". Very little of this ill-health could have been due to diet, because almost without exception people ate natural foods they had provided for themselves, and they were seldom under-nourished.

For instance the farmworker would probably have huge thick slices of bread, doorsteps, spread with dripping for his breakfast, with now and again a boiled egg for a special treat. He would take a couple of slabs of bread for his elevenses, plus a bottle of cold tea. If he was unable to get home for his midday meal, he might have rough sandwiches, with a hunk of cheese and an onion. One exception to this general rule was Zip Mortlocke from the Monument who took the same things every day for his "dinner"— a herring and a lump of cold rice pudding, wrapped up in the same piece of newspaper; winter or summer, wet or fine, Zip sat on the handle of his wheelbarrow in the Pleasure Grounds and ate his herring and rice pudding at midday.

Not a lot of butcher's meat was eaten, it was too expensive, but rabbits were plentiful, cheap and tasty. In fact, they were mostly free, for there were thousands of them in the park—and in the cottage gardens. If you were forced to buy a rabbit, legally, from one of the gamekeepers, you could buy one for fourpence, old money.

Many people had a pheasant at least once a week. If a pheasant came on your garden and ate your peas—well, it was only justice that you should eat the pheasant. There were various ways of catching pheasants; using a fish hook baited with a raisin was the most popular, and the quietest. The only snag was disposing of the feathers; gamekeepers said they could always tell when pheasant feathers were being burned—they probably meant they could tell in which garden they were being burned.

Most people had a joint on Sundays, but it had to last most of the week in various forms. It would be roasted for Sunday and served with Yorkshire (or suet) pudding, and vegetables. The pudding was often—usually, I think—served by itself, with gravy, before the meat course; this took the edge off the appetite, which was a good thing, especially when there were several children in the family.

On Monday the joint, what was left of it, was served cold, with baked or boiled potatoes. On Tuesday slices were warmed up and served with potatoes and vegetables. Today there is a lot of talk about food poisoning due to warmed-up or twice-cooked meat, but I never heard of a case occurring in the village. On Wednesday the bones and remnants of meat still adhering to them were stewed with vegetables and dumplings. Almost every day the meat dish was preceded by a suet pudding.

Thursday was the day for rabbit stew or, if time permitted, rabbit pie, and very tasty it was, too. Sometimes, instead of a rabbit dish, there were sausages or "bangers" made by Mr Wilfred Bonney, the butcher, who lived up the road. Friday was very often fish day, if the fishmonger's cart had been round, and on Saturday we had any sort of made-up meal.

The children who brought sandwiches to school because it was too far for them to go home for their midday meal lived on a diet of starch. Great thick slices of bread thinly spread with jam or dripping or, if they came from a farm, butter. Most of them would have some sort of meal when they returned home, a "hot tea" they called it, not a "high tea"; usually it was warmed up for them in the oven from their father's midday meal.

Cakes, buns and pastries were all home made, and so, of course, was the jam. Tea was the chief drink, with cocoa for the children before going to bed.

There were seasonal foods which were ours for the gathering. Blackberries were in great demand, up to 1st October, on which date the devil was supposed to spit on them and make them uneatable. There were not many to be found in the park, for there were not many bushes or hedges there, but there were a few down Jarvises, some along the "sunk" walk up by the Mowing Ground, and a few in the "goss". The chief source of supply were the hedges along the road and round the fields and meadows; Westley Lane and the Lower Way were the best places. A "chrome" or stick with a curved handle was used to pull down the higher branches.

Mushrooms were another much-prized commodity, but you had to be up very early in the morning to find any of those; by the time we went looking for them they had all been gathered by men going across the park on their way to work. Ice House Hill was the best place for mushrooms, but a few could be found at other places in the park, usually down towards Briar Cottage.

Each family had a garden full of vegetables, and sometimes even plum or greengage trees. There was soft fruit, too, black and red currants, gooseberries, and, not quite so common, strawber-

Nearly every family kept chickens.

ries and raspberry canes. No one ever bought any vegetables; the men worked like slaves in their gardens to keep up a supply of vegetables all the year round. Not many people grew "luxury" fruit or vegetables such as asparagus or tomatoes. Again we were lucky, my father was a keen gardener and had worked for some years under Mr Coster, the head gardener at Ickworth, so we did have strawberries and tomatoes. In fact, we had nearly everything, even asparagus. Each Christmas Mr Coster sent my father a head of celery—really lovely stuff.

Nearly every family kept chickens, but ducks were not so popular as they needed water, and Horringer is a very "dry" place. There were ducks on the farms, of course, and turkeys. One or two people kept geese, but not many. As many people as possible kept a pig, or pigs. There was not so much red tape in those days about where the pig could be kept and quite a lot of people kept them almost on their back doorstep. After all, the smell of "pig" is generally supposed to be healthy. People weren't so fussy in those days.

Our own pigs were killed on the premises, or rather, in the garden. Mr Bonney, the butcher, would appear with his knife; cauldrons of water would be heated; men helpers arrived. There would be frantic piteous squealings, and a few less pitiful but more colourful swear words when one of the helpers slipped over in the muck in the sty. Then silence.

I suppose we must have eaten part of the pig and sold the rest, for no-one had a deep freeze. I can only remember eating the brawn made from the odd bits and pieces, so I expect Mr Bonney bought the carcase; I can't remember.

Most people brewed their own beer. I know my father did up to 1914; I remember the malty smell on the day of the actual brewing, and I remember the upheaval when it was found that the tap to the barrel had been left on. Now and again the bung flew out.

Home-made wine was a "must" for some of the women. The favourite was cowslip, made from flowers picked in Dove's Park, a meadow down Manor Lane; it had the best cowslips around. Dandelion ran it a close second, and goodness knows there were enough dandelions around. Third came parsnip, or maybe elderberry. Having a grape vine in their garden, my aunts next door made grape wine. Later wheat wine became popular; it was as strong as whiskey, even stronger, and was only brought out on special occasions. There were many other varieties of wine made, potato, apple, blackberry and so on.

We did not have many special dishes for special days, apart of course from the usual Christmas fare. For breakfast on Easter Sunday we had boiled eggs, and there were always pancakes on Shrove Tuesday. Round about Christmas we had a surfeit of pheasants and hares; Christmas boxes to my father from the Bristols, Charters, Tollemaches and Simpsons. My father always prepared the hare himself by some mysterious ritual called "jugging" and the result, which we always thought smelt rather odd, was served from a brown earthenware pot like a big jar. No one but my father ate any of it, but we were allowed to clear up the redcurrant jelly which was always served with it.

One special item of food I have not yet mentioned was venison. Every year there was a fawn shoot about October after which it was possible to buy haunches of venison from the gamekeeper. They were too large for one family, so they would be divided among several families. I never could understand why venison was considered such a delicacy in the olden days by Robin Hood and his merry men; I thought it was like tasteless tough mutton.

So, one way or another, Horringer people had a "well-balanced diet", as modern jargon puts it, and were able to withstand all but the fiercest bacteria and germs.

CHAPTER THREE

The Post Office

MY FATHER was the Postmaster at Horringer throughout my childhood so, having lived at the Post Office for thirty-two years, on and off, mostly on, I notice the changes here more than anywhere else.

In the old days, the day began at 5 a.m. when the mail cart arrived from Bury. This was driven by Abraham King, known as "Old Abram", who looked very much like our idea of Father Christmas, with his fresh complexion, fuzz of white hair and frosty blue eyes. He signalled his arrival with a piercing whistle, and my father would go downstairs, unlock the door and take in the bags of mail. I suppose Abram must have got down from the high mail cart to take the bags to the doorstep, but in all the years I never once saw him on the ground; he sat perched up on the high seat looking down on us lesser mortals like a god on the top of Mount Olympus. I have an idea he had a wooden leg—I'm not sure of that, never having seen him get down from his seat.

When Abram had clattered away, my father would go back to bed for another hour. At six o'clock, he would get up and dress and go down and let in the postmen. My mother also got up then to go down and make coffee for all the men, and try to get on with the housework. Usually this was a quiet period, but now and again it was enlivened when Billy Parker had a fit (he was an epileptic); as these fits occurred fairly frequently no one took much notice. My father was quite good at coping with Billy, who usually had his fits in the Post Office and not when he was miles from anywhere in the park.

As well as my father there were three regular postmen; extra ones were taken on for the Christmas rush. The most permanent of these postmen was the aforementioned Billy Parker, who lived with his parents at the village shop—it is now called the Old Stores, as there is a new shop on the St Leonard's Park estate. Billy was small, slow and cheerful, with no compunction whatever at keeping till tomorrow what he did not feel like delivering today. He had a long round, going down to Briar Cottage, across the field (Garden Field) to Slough Lane and Little Horringer Hall, down to

Zoë Leech and her little sister Molly outside the
Post Office which was their home.

27

Mordebois, then he got on to a rough road and went to the Dairy Cottages and Ickworth Lodge. He continued along the road to the Mansion and all round the stable area before going down the hill through the Deer Park, past Ickworth Church to the bothy and gardens. He crossed over the bridge and went along beside the lake. If there were no letters for Martin's Green or the Monument, he carried on until he came to the small round Keeper's Cottage. He continued along the road beside the Fairy Lake, then he could either go across the Mowing Ground, through Jermyn's Clump, and into the stable area, and so back to the village across the park, or he could turn right after passing the Fairy Lake and go through Brickfield Meadow, coming eventually to Bilson's Gate, down the main street, and so home to breakfast.

He made sure that he delivered the mail to Ickworth Lodge and the Mansion regularly, but he was not so fussy about letters and cards for the lesser fry. Surely no one expected him to traipse up to the Monument or Martin's Green with just a postcard; much better to wait until he had two or three items to deliver. No one bothered if an expected communication did not arrive for a few days, or even a week, or even at all; and certainly no one complained if when it did arrive it was a trifle grubby, with fluff, or worse, adhering to it from Billy's pocket. No one complained to my father and they certainly did not write long letters of complaint to the head office in Bury. Imagine what would happen today if a letter was one delivery late. All the busybodies would be writing to head office, the council offices, and there might even be a question asked in Parliament!

Billy was a molecatcher in his spare time, and after he had finished his post round he worked in the park. At least, he was supposed to work, chiefly in the Pleasure Grounds (now called the Acorn Walk), but his hours were very elastic; sometimes he turned up and sometimes he didn't. If he did arrive, he had to recover his strength after doing his round, so most of the rest of the day he sat on the handles of his barrow, probably praying that no one would be foolish enough to send a card or letter to Martin's Green, and adding a postscript to his prayer asking for fine weather.

The second postman, who stayed for several years, was Mr Corbett, who lived in one of the cottages now called West View. He was a retired sergeant-major, or so he said, and he looked the part, with his red face, bristling moustache and choleric temper. He did the up-street round and Salisbury's. He hated having to go to Salisbury's because their cottage was in the middle of a ploughed field, up to the neck in mud in the winter. When a postcard turned up addressed to Salisbury's I have seen Mr Corbett throw the card on the floor, jump on it, yelling with fury, and on the verge of an apoplectic seizure. "Kind regards!" he would shout; "Kind regards!"

The third postman was not so settled. Various men tried the job for a while, but no one seemed to stay very long until after the First World War when George Gooch from Hargrave took on the job. He was a tall good looking ex-guardsman who had been wounded in the war, and he was very popular with us because when he took his money on Fridays he would always give us twopence, and on rare occasions sixpence, if we were around when he was paid. Needless to say, we were there—just by accident, of course. He had the longest round of all, taking the mail out to Chevington and Hargrave in the morning, and bringing their mail back in the evening.

My father did the "down street" round which meant that he went to the two houses down Westley Lane (there were only two then, plus The Cottage), down to Great Horringer Hall and its cottages, back to the village and down Manor Lane, taking in the Rectory and the Manor, and then up to the Hopleys. Apart from very bad weather, he was usually back in time for breakfast at eight o'clock, when the Post Office opened.

My father was a fine singer. Immediately after breakfast he washed and shaved, singing lustily all the while, though his songs were interrupted by splashings and gruntings, but never by swearings. I never once heard my father swear indoors; what he did outside was his own affair. As soon as my father had finished shaving he was gone, either feeding animals or working in the garden.

He was an enthusiastic gardener, and besides the small garden in the front of the Post Office he had a long vegetable garden at the back, and the orchard. Here were a dozen or more apple trees and two walnut trees. He kept hens in the orchard, at one time as many as four hundred. There was no pond, so no ducks, and he did not like geese.

He also kept pigs. There were four sties and these were usually full. The pigs had a habit of getting out, usually when my father was taking a telegram to Hawstead or Chevington. My mother was then faced with the task of catching the pig before it had outrun my father. Usually Mr Salvage, who lived in the School Yard, was able to help, though his legs were no longer than those of the pigs. I think my father lost some of his fondness for pigs when he tripped in one sty and fell face downwards in the bucket of pigs' swill.

Then he had a craze for rabbits—Belgian hares to be exact. I don't know what happened to them, we certainly never ate them.

His departure into the garden and on his rounds left my mother to cope with household chores, cooking the midday meal, plus all

29

the work in the Post Office. Although there were not many pensions or varieties of stamps, there were many more telegrams, as there were no private 'phones in the village.

All these telegrams meant that someone had to deliver them, and that someone was often one of us children, my father being busy in the garden or orchard or pig sties, or even in the process of delivering a telegram somewhere else. Almost before we were able to talk my father drummed into us, "What's in is your own!" A very necessary injunction, as all the news for the big houses came by telegram, and it was very difficult to keep a spicy item of news to oneself!

The Leech family about 1910, in one of those rare moments when the postmaster and his wife were able to relax.

The miles we walked after school, in the holidays or on Saturdays! Our office was responsible for delivering telegrams to other villages when their own offices were closed. Tuesday, I remember, was a day we dreaded, as it was Chevington early closing day, and my father would no sooner be home from one journey out there than he would have to turn round and go there again, and often for a third time. While he was careering round Chevington, we had to take the telegrams for Hawstead, Whepstead, the houses in the park and so on.

One Tuesday afternoon just before Christmas, my father had to take a telegram to Chevington. We arrived home from school (I must have been about nine, as I was still at Horringer School) to find another telegram had come for the same place in Chevington. My mother, thinking to save my father part of the journey, asked me to start walking to meet him. Bessie Salvage, who was ten and who lived with her grandparents in the first cottage in the School Yard (now No 1 Gildhall Cottages), came with me. It must have been about four o'clock when we left home, as it was dark; it was also cold, and a fine sleet was falling. We walked and walked and walked. After the two cottages just beyond Horringer House, there was no other house until we came to Brookes's Corner. We did not meet a living creature all the way along Poulter's Lane. Neither did we meet my father. At Brookes's Corner we turned right towards Chevington, down Weathercock Hill, up Queen Hill, two small girls plodding along in the pitch-black night, soaked to the skin.

Eventually we arrived at Chevington Post Office. Mrs Cooper, when she recovered from her surprise, telephoned my mother to say two drowned rats had arrived, still clutching a telegram; that at least was not wet, as telegrams were always carried in a small black leather pouch slung over the shoulder. Mrs Cooper fed us and dried us while Mr Cooper delivered the telegram, and then he harnessed his horse and took us home in style. We arrived back in Horringer about nine o'clock, yet I seem to remember that no one was very worried about us; Bessie's Granny merely thought we were up to mischief in our garden.

My father had come home down Chedburgh straight road, that was why we had missed him.

We had our favourite places for delivering telegrams. The cottages did not count, as they rarely had any. Among the big houses, the Manor and the Hopleys were prime favourites as they had kind servants who were very generous to small girls. Mrs Steward, the cook at the Manor, was always good for a macaroon or, on special occasions, a crystallised fruit; these were kept in a cupboard just inside the kitchen door. I can see Mrs Steward now, in her pink dress, white apron and cap, from under which her

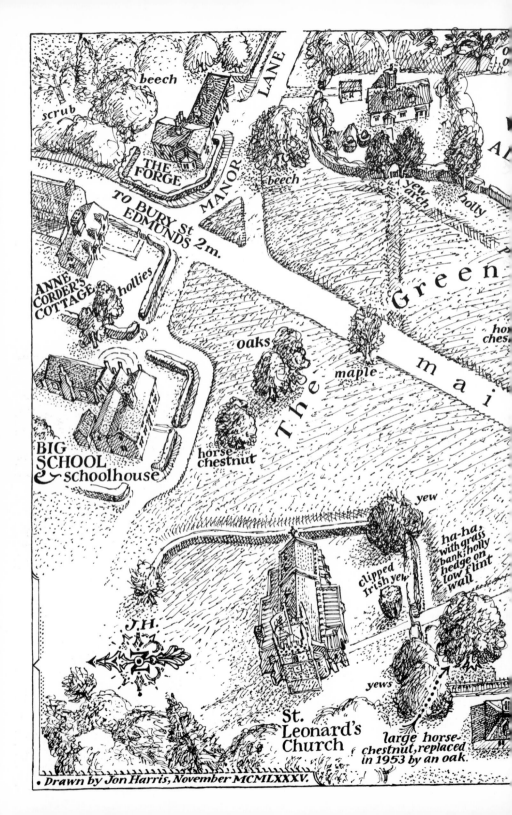

beech

scrub

THE FORGE

beech

MANOR LANE

TO BURY St EDMUNDS 2 m.

yew larch

holly

ANNE CORDER'S COTTAGE

hollies

Green

oaks

maple

The main

horse chest

BIG SCHOOL & schoolhouse

horse chestnut

yew

ha-ha, with grass bank; holly hedge on low flint wall

clipped Irish yew

J.H.

yews

St. Leonard's Church

large horse-chestnut, replaced in 1953 by an oak.

Drawn by Jon Harris, November MCMLXXXV.

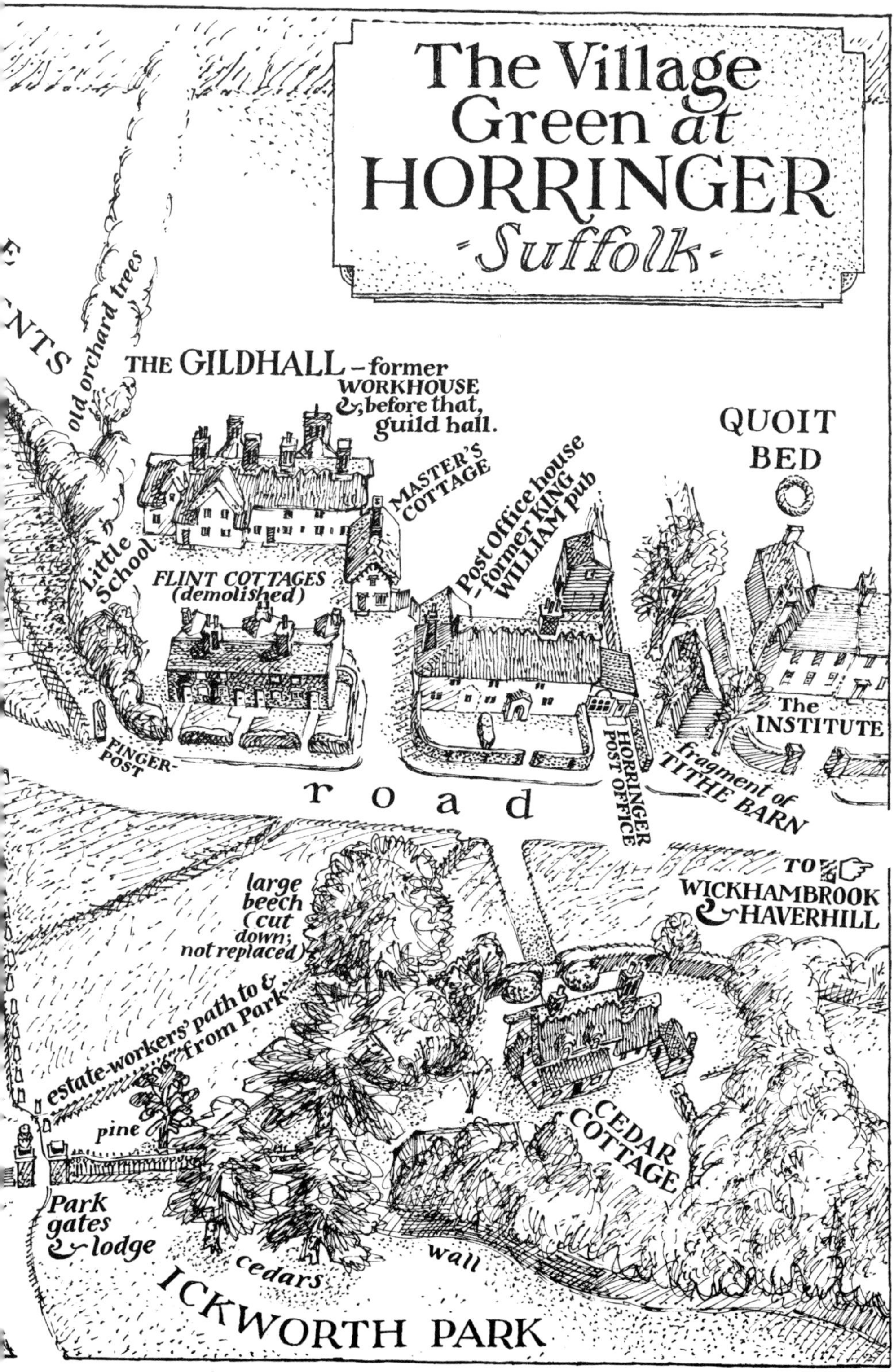

The Village Green at HORRINGER
-Suffolk-

THE GILDHALL – former WORKHOUSE & before that, guild hall.

QUOIT BED

old orchard trees

MASTER'S COTTAGE

Post Office house former KING WILLIAM pub

Little School

FLINT COTTAGES (demolished)

The INSTITUTE

FINGER-POST

HORRINGER POST OFFICE

fragment of TITHE BARN

r o a d

large beech (cut down; not replaced)

TO WICKHAMBROOK & HAVERHILL

estate-workers' path to & from Park

pine

CEDAR COTTAGE

Park gates & lodge

cedars

wall

ICKWORTH PARK

white hair escaped in curls. Miss Marking, cook at the Rectory, was unpredictable, you never knew if you would be given a sweet or a sharp word, and that can be frightening.

I was five when I delivered my first telegram, and when I was seven the joy of taking a telegram to the Manor was rudely shattered. The two enormous (to me) black Labradors were loose, and were hopefully looking in the kitchen window as I rounded the corner of the drive. They heard me, turned, and, uttering what were to me terrifying barks, made for me. I yelled and ran, out of the frying pan into the fire, so to speak—straight into Mr Washington Charters, six-foot-four, sixteen stone, a double-sized edition of choleric Mr Corbet. Had I been less bemused I should have chosen the lesser of two evils and run back to the red slavering jaws of the dogs. As it was, his stentorian roar to the dogs stopped them in their tracks, while he tried to free himself from my clutching hands. I broke away and, still yelling blue murder, did an under-four-minute mile up Manor Lane; I did not stop running or yelling until I reached home, having brought everyone to their doors to see who was being murdered.

To give Mr Charters his due, he came straight up to explain what had happened—how did I know the dogs only wanted to play? They looked like man-eaters to me. Later on, when I read *The Hound of the Baskervilles* I always thought of those two dogs. It was many years before I went to the Manor again, and even today when I go there to a meeting I cast furtive glances at the kitchen window, half expecting to see those black shapes hurtling towards me.

After that incident, taking a telegram to the Hopleys was always fraught with fear. Not only was there the chance of meeting the Manor dogs, but there was also the risk of being dragged down into the spring by the mermaid who was supposed to live in its depths. No one had ever seen her, and looking back I wonder if the story of the mermaid in the spring was told simply to keep us away from the edge. Not that the idea of the mermaid acted as a great deterrent—I can remember many times drinking water from the spring from a laurel leaf cup held under the pipe. The spring, known as St Leonard's Well, must have been a godsend to people walking to or from Bury along the Lower Way.

The Hopleys was the home of the Hon. Mortimer Tollemache, a son of Lord Tollemache of Helmingham Hall. We liked him, he was quiet, courteous and average sized—not like Mr Charters! Another point in their favour was that we were allowed to borrow books from their schoolroom, and that was marvellous for a compulsive reader like myself.

Of course there was a continous stream of telegrams for the Bristols, but the staff at Ickworth were far too superior to take

The Post Office, with Zoë Leech and her sister Molly and a relative standing by the gate.

notice of a small child who had trudged across the Park for about the sixth time in one day. We took the path which led to the stables, through Geraldine's Walk, named after the third Marchioness of Bristol. No dogs, but sometimes the bell stuck and it needed a good deal of effort to make it ring; it was no good knocking on the door, and there was no letter box. Mr Collins, the butler, in spite of his small size, had to be spoken to respectfully, but the footmen were more light-hearted. Of course we always had to wait and see if there was an answer to be taken back; the footmen would ask you in to wait in the hall, but Mr Collins mostly left you standing on the doorstep.

The place I most hated going to was Hawstead Lodge. For one thing it was a long way to walk; for another thing they had dozens of telegrams; and to clinch matters they had several large fierce dogs. I was not really afraid of dogs, but when one is seven or eight years old the animals seem so big.

The walking we did, and very often alone. When I was eleven I had a bicycle, but by then I was at school in Bury and so escaped taking telegrams except on Saturdays, or in the holidays.

When my father joined up in 1915 (leaving my mother to cope with chickens, pigs and rabbits) someone had to be employed to take out the telegrams. Bill Cooper, the nephew of Mr Cooper of

Chevington Post Office, was our first telegraph boy. How he hated taking telegrams from the War Office notifying the next of kin of the death of a husband, son or father; he would open the door, throw the telegram inside, and run.

Back to the Post Office day. There were many customers, chiefly for stamps, because people wrote many more letters in those days. Letters cost a penny, postcards and papers a ha'penny. Friday was the busiest day over the counter, as that was the day the Old Age Pensions were paid out. Horringer had many old people, quite a number of whom could not read or write; they would make their mark, and my mother or one of us would write at the side "John Smith, his mark. E. Leech, witness, Horringer."

One old man—you had to be seventy before you received your pension—said the same thing every Friday when he took his money. "Thank you, ma'am. Thank God and thank Lloyd George."

At noon Abram reappeared and collected the letters which had been posted during the morning. The office did not close for lunch, and I cannot remember that we ever had an uninterrupted meal. My mother sat nearest the door leading into the office, so she went in to serve most often. I was next, so I took my turn as soon as I could see over the counter. When he had finished his meal, my father would go. He used to say that the thing that annoyed him most was when he had to leave a hot meal and go into the office to find a small child there who said, "A ha'penny stamp, please, and mother said would you put it on?" He was also fond of saying that "Women are like slugs—the rain bring them out."

At two o'clock Abram appeared again with more mail for us to deliver. My father had only to deliver along the street and in the Park this time, so he was usually back mid-afternoon. The first part of the afternoon was reasonably quiet, but by teatime the pressure had built up again and after tea it was Bedlam. The telephone rang, children brought letters in, men called on their way home from work, and the postman from Chevington and Hargrave came in, having gone out with his second load just after two o'clock.

Any time after six the private letter bags came in. These were brought by footmen from the Mansion and Ickworth Lodge, and by a male employee from the Manor, the Hopleys and Simpsons at Horsecroft. Each bag had its own key, and my father kept them all hung up on a hook by the letter box. At least that is where they were supposed to be, but they wandered, and then all hell broke loose until they were found.

About half an hour before old Abram was due again (he came at eight o'clock before the 1914–18 war, at seven o'clock afterwards) the sealing wax saucepan would be put on the oil stove in the kitchen, the dried sealing wax in the saucepan being augmented by extra pieces chipped from a long stick of sealing wax. What a smell there was as the wax warmed up! The warming wax occasionally boiled over, or caught fire, or the stove smoked; then there was a flurry of activity, the saucepan was thrown out into the garden to cool, and after a decent interval the whole process began again, ending when the wax was melted enough for a dollop to be put on the knots of the string tying the mailbags, each dollop being firmly stamped with the official brass seal. Every day there were at least two mailbags, one for letters and one for parcels.

Abram arrived more or less punctually at eight o'clock. During the earlier evening various people (men, of course) dropped in to discuss village matters with my father—why the cricket team had lost their last match, who would be chosen to play for the quoit team, and so on. I remember one memorable incident connected with this get-together which happened early in November; half a dozen men, including the village policeman, were in the office for their nightly session of putting the village to rights when there was a loud bang outside. The door blew open, the lamp blew out and for a second or so there was pandemonium, then P.c. Avey came out of his trance, shot out a long arm and grabbed a stunned Derek Potter by the collar, hauling him in to face six large men. Never in his wildest dreams could Derek have hoped to achieve such success as the result of putting one small banger on the doorstep! He had been so stunned by the result of his enterprise

The Post Office and the neighbouring cottages as they were when the author was a girl.

that he had forgotten to run—hence his ignominious capture. Not even the look of injured innocence on his angelic face, nor his protestations that "Please it wasn't me, it was the others" saved him from a jolly good clip on the ear from more than one of the shaken gathering.

Eight o'clock, the mail gone, the lamp was blown out, the office door locked, and another day was over. Fifteen hours' work, five and a half days a week, for about two pounds, and no pension at the end of it, except the Old Age Pension.

That was a typical day, but there were variations. On Saturday nights the weekly accounts had to be done, and on Sunday nights alterations to the Post Office rules had to be stuck in the Rule Book. At the end of the month gloom descended on the house when the monthly accounts had to be done, they never came right the first time.

Sunday was not a day of rest, either. The office was open until

A sketch map showing the rounds walked by the postmen.

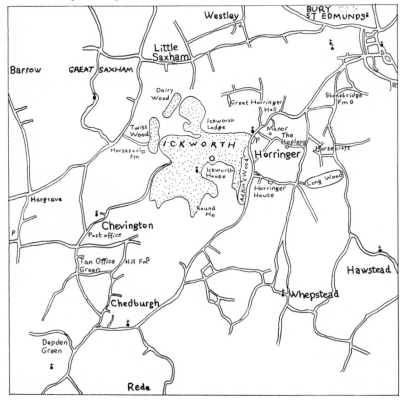

ten o'clock for business and telegrams. On alternate Sundays my father had to cycle to Chevington, Hargrave, back across Depden Green, through to Whepstead, and so home, clearing the pillar boxes en route, with luck arriving home in time to get the letters stamped and tied up ready to be picked up by Abram in the mailcart at six. On alternate Sundays the round was done by George Gooch or whoever was doing it daily. We could never go out together on a Sunday, as someone always had to be at home to attend to the mailman.

Christmas, of course, was a period of intense activity. About a week before the rush started my mother would cook a huge ham, and we practically lived on that until Christmas Day. She also made a huge quantity of mincepies and sausage rolls, chiefly for the postmen and the extra men taken on during the rush. The weather was bad, the mailcart was late, there were hundreds of letters and cards to be sorted; Billy Parker invariably had a fit; the postmen were late setting out; all the morning people were coming in for stamps or with parcels; the mailcart was late at midday; the postmen came back in time to sort out a second delivery, snatch a bite, and go off again. The afternoon was hectic and the men would all be late back, but that did not matter because Abram was later; and all the time the telephone was ringing, piles of telegrams awaited delivery, and the stream of customers continued unabated.

Christmas was not spread over such a long period in those days. All the extra work was compressed into one week; and how exhausted everyone was at the end. We never really enjoyed our Christmasses; my father and mother were tired out, and we all had an extra burden to bear in the shape of my father's mother, a headmistress somewhere (I've forgotten where), who descended on us as soon as her school closed and expected to be fed at regular intervals—she just sat and waited and never did a hand's turn to help. She considered she was above such menial work as washing up—and we children kept out of her way as much as we could.

Like everyone else in the village we had relations and friends in for tea on Christmas Day and Boxing Day, the only two days' holiday allowed. After an enormous tea we settled down to various games and a sing-song. Our regular Christmas guests were the Salvages; Amos Salvage was a gardener at Ickworth, a small round brown man, who always wore a crimson waistcoat, making him look like a robin. His garden adjoined our orchard and my father was continually in disgrace as his hens and other animals always thought the vegetables in Amos's garden were better than those in ours; it was easy to get through the hedge, and the sight of Amos chasing a large fat sow gave us great pleasure.

He always sang to us at Christmas. Mellowed by home-made

A view of the Green, with the forge on the left from which help could be obtained when the Post Office was especially busy.

wine, he was inclined to let bygones be bygones and so treated us to his stock in trade, "Little Polly Perkins of Paddington Green" and "Barbara Allen". My mother slept during the recital, my aristocratic grandmother looked disapproving, my father tried to look polite, one of my aunts who had hopes (which were not fulfilled) of becoming a second Mrs Salvage applauded loudly, and Amos's daughter tried to look as though he didn't belong to her.

My father, a great sportsman (he was playing cricket for Horringer when he was seventy), had a suspect knee from the days he played football. This knee had a horrible habit of "going out" at the most inopportune moments, and my father then had to take to his bed until the doctor came and put it in again. He had a cartilage operation when he was over fifty, but it didn't seem to do much good. When he was laid up, or when my mother was ill and my father had to stay in to look after the office, a job he hated, someone had to be found to do his rounds. A very present help in trouble was Mr Dennis Marriott, of the forge, who always seemed to be able to lend a hand, sometimes for weeks at a time. He was quite near to be called on if telegrams piled up when the regular "deliverers" were already out on the job; three blasts on my

40

mother's whistle told him he was urgently needed. There were times when my mother was frantic to find someone to help and had to go out into the highways and hedges and compel the lame, the halt and the blind to come to her aid.

How honest and conscientious these "roped in" people were! The children thought it was "something" to be asked to deliver a telegram, and were delighted with the penny they received. Grown-ups were glad to earn sixpence or even a shilling to deliver a long distance (Chevington or Whepstead) telegram. There were fixed payments for delivering telegrams, based on the mileage, but naturally we children were not paid—we owned the firm, so to speak.

The regular postmen were most conscientious. Rain, hail, snow, gales, muddy roads, heat, frost, they struggled on. I can remember hearing of only one postman who broke under the strain, a man who walked the Chevington–Hargrave round. One evening, footsore and weary, he plodded down Poulter's Lane in the dark and wet; suddenly it dawned on him that he would be doing the same tomorrow, the next day, and the next. Taking the mail he had collected out of the canvas postbag, he threw all the letters, cards and so on into the ditch by the side of the road, marched into the Post Office, banged the bag down on the counter, said to my father "I'm through!" and walked out. My father had to get on his bicycle and ride along Poulter's Lane until he found the sodden letters and cards in the ditch.

There were funny incidents I can remember too. There was the time my sister sent her teddy bear to Bury in the mailbag; and the time she filled her pockets with silver from the cash box and gave it to Boy Collins, saying cheerfully "You have it, we've got plenty more at home."

After the First World War the winds of change began to blow, and today there is very little of the old regime left. About 1928 the mailcart was replaced by a mailvan, and old Abram's whistle by a toot on the horn. Just at the time the change was made there was one of those scares about the world coming to an end on a certain day, a story which was accepted hook, line and sinker by a teacher then lodging in the village, and when the mail van arrived with a loud toot on the horn she was convinced that the day of doom had come. She rushed downstairs and out on to the green expecting to find it filled with hosts of angels—but all she saw was a small red van.

The postmen are all gone, even the postwoman (past person, perhaps I should say) who delivered mail along the street and St Leonard's Park has ceased her rounds; all mail is now delivered by the mail van which comes out at seven instead of five in the morning. A second van comes out about eleven, and one goes back at 11.20 a.m.. The evening mail goes out at 5.25 p.m. At the moment there is no Sunday collection at all. The office hours are different too. Opening time is 9 a.m.; there is a break from one to two for lunch, and the office closes for the day at 5.30 p.m. except on Wednesdays, when it does not re-open after lunch. The weekend closure is from noon on Saturday till Monday morning.

Three weeks' holiday is allowed nowadays provided someone can be found to stand in; I can remember us having only one holiday, a fortnight in Bournemouth. No telegrams come through the village Post Office now; most people receive theirs over the 'phone, and the few for those who have no telephone are delivered by a telegraph boy on a motor-cycle. There is a telephone kiosk by the Post Office, used chiefly by lorry drivers passing through. Increased postal charges have cut down the amount of mail, and very few people can afford to post parcels, though there is a small business in air mail letters.

It is much quieter in the Post Office now without the comings

Mordebois Cottages, which were on Billy Parker's long round.

and goings of the postmen and the continual ringing of the telephone; no footmen bring in letter bags these days. Letter writing is dying out because people find it is quicker to use the telephone.

Confectionery, stationery, cigarettes, crisps, birthday cards, magazines, papers and "lights" are sold at the Post Office now, and Mrs Bumstead organises a newspaper round for the village. As there are so many more children in the village owing to development, and they all have so much money to spend, a brisk trade is done out of school hours in sweets and similar commodities. A sign of the times is the large glass and steel grille which has been installed between the customer and the postmistress, a horrible thing but necessary in these days of thuggery and vandalism.

In spite of the long hours, the hundreds of telegrams we used to handle and the Christmas rush, I think there is something to be said for the "good old days" after all.

Pheasant Cottage, the pride of Horringer Street—then and now.

CHAPTER FOUR

The Church and Parson

EVERYONE WENT to church on Sundays. Those who could not get to the morning service went to the one in the evening; most children were dragged there twice a day. There were few chapel people and no Roman Catholics in the village.

There was a service for the people of Ickworth in their church in the park every Sunday morning. This service was attended by the Bristol family and their house guests, and those of their staff who could be spared; by the Bevans who were living at Ickworth Lodge at that time, their staff, and all the other people who were living in the park.

Lord Manners Hervey, brother of the fourth Marquis of Bristol and rector of Horringer and Ickworth from 1900 to 1944, was picked up at his rectory in Horringer round about 9.30 on Sunday mornings by a groom driving a pony trap. A few minutes before ten, when the service at Ickworth Church began, the Bristols arrived and went into their own gallery pew. On the rare occasions when we went to Ickworth Church we were herded into the children's gallery, from where we could look over into the Bristols' pew and down into the body of the church.

There was a harmonium to accompany the singing, played by various people, Mrs White, the gamekeeper's wife, Miss Coster from the gardens, or, in an emergency, by Lord Manners himself. There was no choir.

We preferred Ickworth Church for some reason, maybe because we knew the sermon would be brief as Lord Manners had to be back in Horringer in time for the eleven o'clock service there. Sometimes Lord Manners had a curate to help him conduct the service at Ickworth; he always had a curate to help him with the morning and evening service at Horringer Church, and some-times he had a "guinea-man" from Cambridge to help the curate—a gentleman of the cloth who had no parochial duties and was able to help out with services at a guinea (£1.05) a time.

My father was a great churchman, and being in the Horringer Church choir he rarely missed a service. His many preparations on the Sunday morning began when his best suit, usually dark grey or black, was brought downstairs and draped over the back

The tower of Horringer Church, seen through the churchyard gate.

of a chair in front of the fire in the living room; the shirt with its stiff white front and stiff collar was aired in front of the fire in the kitchen.

After breakfast, he really got down to it. Having already washed once, he washed again, then shaved, after "stropping" his cut-throat razor; and all the while he sang. He had a fine tenor voice, and on Sunday mornings we were treated to a rehearsal of the hymns we would hear in church that day, and which he had sung at choir practice the previous Friday night. Having finished his repertoire of hymns, he would sing some of his favourite songs, such as *Queen of Angels, Ora pro nobis,* or *Trumpeter, what are you sounding now?* On weekdays he sang songs like *Any old iron,* and *Wire in, my lads.* The house really resounded with his singing.

When he had shaved, he collected his clothes from in front of the fires and betook himself upstairs to dress. He wore gold cuff-links on Sundays and a tiepin with a diamond in it. He always looked very dapper, even putting pomade on his moustache.

The interior of Horringer Church, with the oil lamps which would sometimes go out if the pew was jogged.

We children were sent to the ten o'clock Sunday School, which was held in the Infants' School. There were various teachers, usually the Bevan daughters from Ickworth Lodge. Frances Bevan was tall and dark, and Katherine, who later perished with her family in a fire at her home in Kent, was plump and more easy going. They were a very unlucky family.

At a quarter to eleven when the church bells began to chime, or ring on special occasions, we went across the green to Horringer Church, being joined on the way by a contingent of older children who had been taught in the "Big School". We all marched up to the area by the organ where there were benches for us, and where we were out of the way of the main congregation and under the eagle eye of John Willie, the headmaster of the "Big School", who was playing the organ. The really young ones were allowed to leave before the sermon, the rest of us soldiered on. If any adults in the family were attending morning service (it was not called matins in those days) we were allowed to sit with them and not with the Sunday School.

The chancel has been so altered and re-arranged since Lord Manners' day that I find it rather difficult to sort out, but I will do my best to describe the layout of the church. There were four pews in the chancel, just beyond the step, two pews on each side, reserved for the more important people in the parish. Those occupying these four pews came into church by the side door which led straight into the chancel. The family living at Horsecroft House had their own small Horsecroft Chapel, the door to which is in the main porch. It was built in the fifteenth century and seems always to have been considered "the sole property" of those at Horsecroft.

In the chancel there was a gangway between the four pews and the choir stalls, occupied by a large all-male choir, at least twelve men and as many boys. The tenors sat in the back row, and the altos in front of the organ. Lord Manners sat at the end of their row, and the curate, usually a Mr Mills at that time, sat at the end of the row of tenors. The choir wore black cassocks and white surplices, but they did not wear ruffs until about 1946.

The nave of the church was occupied by the rest of the congregation, usually fifty or sixty people.

In spite of the church being heated by hot water pipes and radiators it was never very warm. Lighting was by oil lamps, a dozen of them, each one attached to a metal pole which was held more or less stable by passing through a hole in the prayer-book shelf. An accidental jog on the hymn-book ledge would not only cause a loud vibration but would cause the lamp to flicker and smoke, and sometimes to go out. There was never a dull moment during the service in those days; we children were always hopeful that something exciting would happen, and it very often did.

Few women came to the morning service as they had the Sunday dinners to cook; they used to come to Evensong, when the church would be even better filled than in the morning, despite the absence of the V.I.P.s who had their own dinners in the evening. For some reason I always preferred the evening service; perhaps it was because the curate or the guinea-man usually preached and we could understand them better than we could Lord Manners. The choir were there in force again, having got their second wind, and the service by the light of the flickering lamps was something not easily forgotten.

The church festivals, too, were something to remember. On the three chief ones, the Sunday before Christmas, Easter Day and Harvest Festival, the church was packed to the doors; Whitsunday was not so popular. On all these occasions the church was beautifully decorated and looked even more delightful in the soft lamplight than in the sunlight of the morning. A great deal of the colour was taken away when the east window depicting Matthew, Mark, Luke and John was replaced by the present anaemic-looking one about 1946.

Easter, perhaps, showed the church at its prettiest—daintiest would perhaps be a better word. The predominant colours in the decorations were yellow and white, with daffodils in profusion and white narcissi. The window ledges on the north side became mossy carpets on which nestled bunches of violets, and on the altar stood vases of Madonna lilies; very attractive they looked. We had been prepared for the Easter services by those held on Palm Sunday, when one of the hymns in the morning was always *All glory, laud and honour,* and in the evening the quieter, sadder *Ride on, ride on, in majesty.* Needless to say our house had resounded to those hymns all the week.

The greatest Sunday of all was without doubt Harvest Festival Sunday, usually towards the end of September. Although by six-thirty, the time of the evening service, the brightness of the day was beginning to fade, those who came to the service had only one journey, and that the homeward one, to make in darkness. Everyone came to that evening service. If you wanted a seat you had to go early, in fact you had to be in the church by six at the latest, for by quarter past six every seat was occupied; chairs were placed down each aisle and even up in the chancel. Very often more chairs had to be rushed over from the Parish Room in the Rectory, and sometimes latecomers stood in the belfry. Many more men than usual were in the congregation, as most of them were employed on the land.

On either side of the main door was a large sheaf of corn, and smaller sheaves were placed at each end of the altar. Bunches of

Ickworth Church, which was attended by the Bristols and their house guests every Sunday morning.

corn were tied under the lamp on each lamp post. There were loaves of bread, home-made, on the altar, and the pulpit, font, lectern and window ledges were ablaze with asters, dahlias, michaelmas daisies and other autumn flowers. At the base of the font and among the flowers on the window ledges were dozens of shining apples, and usually two or three enormous marrows were placed at strategic points in the church.

At the beginning of both the Harvest Festival services the choir walked in procession round the church, and again at the end. We had all the usual harvest hymns, the first one was always *Come ye thankful people come.* Then we sang *We plough the fields and scatter the good seed on the land; Praise O praise our God and King,* and *To thee, O Lord our hearts we raise,* followed by *The sower went forth sowing,* and as a sop to the children present, *Fair waved the golden corn.*

Of course there was an anthem, during the singing of which the congregation sat and recovered its breath. Even the sermon did not seem as long as usual; there was so much colour to absorb, and the starched white surplices of the choir really glistened "whiter than white" among the flowers.

Then out into the cool darkness of the autumn night, a wait in the porch or at the church gate for Father, who was either pleased with or critical of the anthem, a brisk walk across the green, and so home to bed.

The church bells pealed on such occasions. The village was very proud of its team of bellringers, who were all middle-aged men. As far as I can remember they did not have a regular practice night, for which those of us living near the church were thankful. Having a peal of eight bells, two being added to the original six in

49

St Leonard's Church, Horringer, seen from the Green at the time of which Mrs Ward is writing.

1912 in memory of Lord Arthur Hervey, Bishop of Bath and Wells, son of the first Marquis of Bristol and rector of Ickworth from 1832–1869, our belfry was in great demand and teams of ringers from all over the country would come to ring the bells in Horringer Church. They did not come often, and did not seem to stay as long as visiting teams do now—or else we were playing down the park or somewhere out of earshot!

Lord Manners Hervey was the brother of the fourth Marquis of Bristol and nephew of the third marquis, so it was obvious that he would be rector of Horringer and Ickworth as soon as he was ordained. In appearance he was tall, about six feet, a typical Hervey with a pale ascetic face and blue eyes, and he usually wore a trilby which made him appear even taller than he really was. He was always impeccably turned out, with dazzling linen; he was waited on hand and foot by two devoted servants, Miss Anne Marking the cook and Miss Emily Walker the housemaid. They adored him, and delighted in seeing that everything ran smoothly for him for the forty-four years he was rector.

There was also a gardener, Mr Walter Sturgeon, who lived with his family in a cottage which is now part of "The Gables" in Manor Lane. He was helped by a boy, and together they kept the large garden immaculate; the lawns were like velvet, and no weed dared to show itself in the flower beds, while the large kitchen garden was a joy to behold with its neat rows of vegetables and

50

well-pruned fruit trees. Lord Manners had a great interest in his garden, particularly in his rock garden and the small pond beside it. He would spend hours weeding the garden, and was continually adding to it until he must have had one of the finest rock gardens in the country.

He was a man of considerable learning, a fact which his parishioners did not appreciate, particularly as he tended to visit them at the most inconvenient moments, usually when a meal had just been put on the table. He would sit and talk learnedly on Byzantine architecture or Battersea enamel or some such subject while the food got cold. His sermons, too, were far above the heads of his congregation. He bought them so many at a time and read them to us from the pulpit; now and again he got the pages mixed, and when that happened he finished off in a hurry.

Lord Manners was very musical—he played the piano and the organ—and while he was rector the choir flourished, but some of the men left in the late nineteen-twenties when he decided to add women and girls to the choir. The men, my father among them, said they left because Lord Manners introduced a new system of "pointing" in the psalms, but that was not the real reason! There were some very good sopranos among the women in the village but the general exodus of men and boys spoilt a really good choir.

My father did not go to church regularly again. Instead he spent his Sunday mornings rabbiting and ratting with Charlie Charters, the black sheep of the Charters family, who had two lovely cream ferrets which he carried round inside his shirt.

Lord Manners was fond of saying that the fool of the family was always made a parson. He won only one prize when he was at school, he used to say, and when he went up to receive it from his headmaster the latter said "You have not won this prize because you are so good, but because the others are so bad!"

One of his interests was local history, and in 1930 he published at his own expense his book *The Annals of a Suffolk village—a history of Horringer*. He would talk to anyone on this subject, but unfortunately not many people were interested and a lot of his knowledge died with him.

In many ways easily taken in, he was naive and trusting and was often conned with a hard luck story—usually a tissue of lies. There was a good deal of talk about the way he disbursed the charity money, because it was reckoned that he would fall for any "smarmy" person, a weakness which exasperated Miss Marking and Emily.

As the years passed he became very deaf and absent minded. One misty December afternoon in 1944 he walked across the road in front of a lorry carrying Italian prisoners of war and was hit by the lorry. He died in hospital a day or two later.

Horningsheath
1914
Sts 2

CHAPTER FIVE

The Schools

UP TO 1942 there were two schools in the village, the Infant School in what was until recently the School Yard (I don't know what it is called now—the Gildhall, I suppose), and the "Big School" as it was called, across the green where the only village school is now.

The "Infant" or "Little School", built on to the end of the Gildhall or Workhouse about 1846, was originally a boys' school, the girls and infants being taught in the school across the green. Later this was changed, the infants going to the school in the School Yard and the older girls and boys to the Big School.

It was to the Infant or "Little School" we went at the age of five, or before if it could be wangled. Living so near, I used to slip in long before I was five, only to be ignominiously hauled out by someone who had been sent to look for me.

There were, on average, thirty-six children in attendance at the "Little School" when I reached the mature age of five and could be admitted. I do not think there were any children under five attending when I first started; I do not see how they could have been crammed in, we were packed in like sardines as it was. The one room was divided into two parts by a green baize curtain. The babies were taught by Teacher Flo, or to give her her proper name, Miss Florence Garwood, in the first section of the room; the older infants were taught by the headmistress, Mrs "Toff" Cooke, in the other section of the room.

The room was not equally divided—the babies had about a third of the room, the "top class" had two-thirds; the one fireplace was in Mrs Cooke's room, the one door was in Teacher Flo's room. Consequently, what with no real heat being felt from the fire and the door being continually opened and shut as children went to the toilets across the playground, and with visitors, officials and parents coming in at all times, the babies' section was like an icehouse in winter. As most children wore a lot of clothes in the winter, "six flannel petticoats and camphorated oil," and as some were sewn into their underclothes for the winter, perhaps they did not feel the cold.

Zoë Leech, on the right of the front row, and some of her schoolfellows.

Teacher Flo, who always wore a stiffly starched white embroidered pinafore, had graduated from being a monitor to being recognised as a supplementary teacher. These supplementary teachers were unqualified and not eligible for a pension, but Teacher Flo was marvellous with homesick new entrants, and the average child could read, write and do arithmetic before moving to the other side of the curtain; and they knew their tables.

Teacher Flo was very much in awe of Mrs Cooke. "Frightened to death of her, I was," she told me the other day.

We little ones used sand trays for making our letters in to begin with, then we were given slates. The joy of making a pencil squeak—quite accidentally, of course! We had wooden bricks to play with, and plasticine, and we threaded innumerable beads on to pieces of string. Much of our time was spent outside when the weather permitted, either in the playground or, as a treat, in the

Teacher Flo.

park, where we would sit in a circle under a tree while Teacher Flo read to us or while we recited poems to her.

I don't remember learning to read; I must have learnt before going to school. All I know is that reading lessons bored me to tears.

In spite of the fact that it was colder at the back of the room there was great competition to get there, because it was then possible to peep round the curtain at the other class and make faces at the person who was sitting by the curtain on that side. A certain amount of care was needed, as not everyone liked being the butt of one of the babies, and there was always the chance of hearing a shout, "Please ma'am, so and so is looking round the curtain!" Retribution was swift.

At last the great and rather dreaded day came when we moved "up", or rather through the curtain. Gone were the carefree days of sand trays and bead frames and friendly chats. Being able to see the fire was no substitute for Teacher Flo's kindness; Mrs Cooke was a very different cup of tea. She was prim and proper, and very strict, and when she used the cane, which she did frequently, she really laid it on. I was only caned once, for talking. I was six at the time.

Although I was never in trouble about my work, I never got on well with Mrs Cooke. To begin with, she had favourites, and the chief of these was her niece Iris, or Babs as she was known. When Mrs Cooke chose the cast for one of the small plays she was so fond of producing Iris always had the chief part and her friends the other roles. To add to our grievance the "play" was always performed right in front of the fire, and we had to sit and shiver while those performing were scorching. My friend Barbara Collins—daughter of the butler at Ickworth—and I were never

Teachers and pupils of the Infants' School at the time Zoë Leech was a pupil. Mrs Cooke is on the left of the back row and Teacher Flo on the right. The children are:
Back row: Iris (Babs) Cooke, Fred Rosier, Cissie White, T. Bullass, Alice Bumstead, Frances Baker, Orby Ramsey and Reginald Corbett.
Second row: Zoë Leech, Kenneth Cooke, Freddie Palmer, Douglas White, Winnie Harper, unknown, May Salisbury, Ruby Ramsey, unknown.
Third row: Maisie Talbot, Jack Barkham, Percy Last, Ivy Boreham, Daisy Sturgeon, Arthur Barkham, Josiah Ashman, unknown, Barbara Collins.
Front row: Sidney Matthews, Bill Last, Tom Lloyd, Winnie Sewell, Bessie Salvage, Edith Boreham, Mildred Peake and Hector Smith.

chosen, and how I hankered to take part and to use the tiny china tea service which was always produced on those occasions.

Barbara and I could do our schoolwork—all but needlework, and my goodness, didn't that please Mrs Cooke! I'll admit my dirty, sticky "specimen" was revolting, and it was never finished, but what I suffered at that teacher's hands is beyond telling! Full marks for reading, writing and arithmetic counted for naught—I couldn't sew, and that was good enough for her.

At seven we moved over the green to the "Big" school. Barbara being slightly older moved before I did, so I was left to cope on my own. However, after a month or so, I followed Barbara into the maelstrom of a hundred boys and girls up to fourteen years of age. "Babs" did not follow us until a year later.

The headmaster was John Matthew Buckmaster Curtis, who had been appointed in 1897. He came from Norfolk, and was never tired of comparing Norfolk with Suffolk—always to the detriment of Suffolk.* He was a tall upright soldierly looking man, and we little ones, and many of the big ones as well, were terrified of him. He had two assistants; Miss Lily Coster, who was the daughter of the head gardener at Ickworth, and who taught the sevens and eights, and another teacher who took the nines and tens. Mr Curtis, known to the unregenerate as "John Willie", took all the rest. The slower learners, of whom there were plenty, never got as far as the top class—either by cunning on the part of John Willie or cunning on the part of the dullards.

Miss Coster taught her class in the small room, while the "middle" teacher and John Willie shared the main room. Needless to say, the one fireplace was nearer John Willie's end. There was no partition or curtain separating these two classes, and that may have been the reason for the quick turnover of staff for that middle class, especially as John Willie taught his class as though he was alone in the room. There were thirty plus in each class, so there would be sixty to seventy children in that top room. The three teachers I can remember for that middle class were Miss Eppy, a farmer's daughter from Whepstead; Miss Ada Frost, who cycled daily from Bury; and a Miss Margaret Thompson, who lodged in the village.

Miss Coster, who was fair with blue eyes and a lovely complexion, had the small room on her own, and a lovely time we had, always keeping a wary eye on the glass partition in case John Willie was on the prowl. She was a good teacher, her father and my father were friends, and she liked bright children, so life was easy and happy—mostly. She took needlework throughout the school, Miss Frost took the middle boys for art, and John Willie

---

*Mr Curtis was headmaster until 1926. He died in 1960 at the age of ninety-nine.

Mr J. M. B. Curtis.

Miss Lily Coster.

took the senior boys for gardening; he was a very good gardener. While Miss Coster was taking another class for needlework and Miss Frost was taking art, someone had to take Miss Coster's class, and there was great competition among the senior girls to do this. I was never a senior, leaving for Bury School when I was eleven, so I never "took the class."

The system of promotion was very fluid, and I was in "the master's class" by the time I was nine, so I can't have stayed long in Miss Frost's class, which was rather a pity as she was quiet and peaceful. It must have been a great strain for her teaching in the same room as John Willie, who was not the quietest of teachers; he must have had eyes in the back of his head, because he could see what was going on in his class and in Miss Frost's at the same time.

Twice while I was in Miss Coster's class I was sent for by John Willie to go and read to the top class, and that did not make me very popular with my classmates, I can tell you. However, pride goes before a fall, and any pride I might have had was quickly erased when it came to the needlework lesson. We always seemed to be making aprons of stiff white calico, and the main part had to be gathered into a band.

One memorable day, I suppose I was eight or nine, my mother decided to take my sister and me, Barbara and Boy Collins, and Gwen and Lance Avey (the policeman's daughters), to Bury to the pictures, which was a treat of tremendous proportions, in spite of our having to walk to Bury and back. How slowly the afternoon

A bowler-hatted Mr J. M. B. Curtis, known to his pupils as John Willie, with pupils of the "Big School" in 1914.
Back row: Jack Rowe, Arthur Grainger, Jack Honeyball, Ernie Potter, unknown, Walter Cooke and Bert Barkham.
Middle row: Mary Hunt, Dolly Smith, Nesta Kitcatte, Freda Rosier, Ruth Hart, Daisy Cooke and Mabel Sargent.
Front row: Florrie Gooch, Bessie Salvage, Bob Sturman, Ken Cooke, Jack Corbett, Douglas White and Olive Peake.

went, and how often we looked out of the window to see if it was keeping fine.

It was needlework afternoon, and I had progressed as far as "stroking" my gathers and putting them into the band on my apron—goodness knows how I had got that far! I worked like a slave, and the band on my apron was decorated all along with tiny spots of blood from my pricked fingers, for the calico was stiff and my hands were small.

At last the band was on—a memento of "blood, toil, tears and sweat," and I proudly took it out to Miss Coster. She gave it one contemptuous look, pulled at the band and the gathers broke!

"Go back to your seat and do it again," she said. In a fury because all my hard work was wasted, and I had been so proud of it, I said "I shan't!"

I don't know who was the most surprised, Miss Coster, the class, or myself.

"You will stay behind until you apologise to me," she said.

So I went back to my place, clutching the shredded apron. And I sat.

I think the school closed at ten to four. Anyway, I am not sure of the time—it seemed an eternity to me. The rest of the class left, though my sister did make an effort on my behalf, saying to Miss Coster "But we're going to the pictures!"

"She will go when she apologises to me for her rudeness!" said Miss Coster.

The school emptied. Miss Frost put on her hat and cardigan, got out her bicycle, and rode away. John Willie came down and spoke to Miss Coster in a low voice. Then he left, and the school cleaner came in.

Presently I heard chattering from outside, and recognised the voices of the cinema party, who were obviously speaking loudly for my benefit. "There is still time for you to go with them," said Miss Coster, not unkindly.

I made no reply, but just sat. How I hated her, and that dirty bedraggled apron! By four-thirty I realised that although I had lost my treat, nothing worse could happen to me and Miss Coster was obviously wishing to be away. So I sat, feeling slightly more cheerful about it.

At five o'clock she called it a day and told me to go. Head high, I walked out of the room, closed the door with exaggerated care, then fled across the playground and the green.

There was no sympathy for me at home, of course, but when I returned to school the next day, I found myself something of a heroine as the one "who had kept old Lily at school till five!" Needless to say, from then until I left there was no love lost between Miss Coster and myself! I can't remember what happened to the cause of it all, that dirty, blood-stained apron. Used as a duster I should think.

Being in John Willie's class was like sitting on the edge of a volcano. How that man worked! He never eased up for one minute, and his discipline was rigid. But his weak point was his fear of offending some of the parents. Some he did not mind offending, of course, but I have seen him give sixpence (or an apple) to someone whose ears he had boxed—Barbara Collins

Horringer school and some of its pupils in Edwardian times.

once had sixpence, I remember—as a bribe so they should not tell their fathers. Barbara's crime was writing a "love letter" to Hector Smith which John Willie intercepted and read aloud to the enthralled class. The note read, "Dear Hector, I love you. Do you love me?" Hector never spoke to her again after saying coldly that it was nothing to do with him. Poor Barbara! I don't think she ever lived that down.

John Willie had his hands full with a huge class of boys and girls, and some of the fourteen-year-old boys were as big as he was. He gave us a good grounding in essentials, and while he was working with one group he gave the other groups chunks of poetry to learn. I remember getting sixpence from him for reciting a hundred and ninety-six lines of Scott's *Lay of the Last Minstrel* to him without a mistake—"The way was long, the wind was cold!"

So was the classroom! It really paid to be a nuisance because then you were put in the front row where he could reach you with the cane, but at least you were warm, unless the fire smoked, which it usually did, or you were on the end of the row near the gangway between the classes, where the wind whistled under the

60

door. I left before I reached the far end of his room which was reserved for the thirteen and fourteen-year-olds, but it must have been mighty cold up there. As I have said before, the children wore many more clothes than they do today, and they needed them! Most of them wore knitted woollen cuffs on their wrists in the winter, and some suffered terribly from chilblains.

Having an age range of from seven to fourteen, there was bound to be a certain amount of bullying, especially between the big fourteen-year-old boys and the small girls. Usually the sevens and eights were let out of school before the older ones and so were able to get away before being pounced on, but occasionally we were caught and had our hair pulled, our legs and arms struck with nettles, or our tormentors resorted to some other refinement of torture. The two worst bullies were Arthur Grainger (finished up as a major in the Army) and "Rinky" Debenham, and until they left school I was terrified of them.

Although John Willie ruled with a rod of iron, he was unable to subdue everyone. I remember on one occasion Jack Rowe ran out of the school, jumped the gate and legged it to freedom, hotly pursued by an irate J.W. brandishing the cane. Someone caught Jack as he sped across the green and returned him by the hair to J.W. We enjoyed that.

Fred or "Spitty" Palmer attacked from behind. John Willie was leading us in from a session on the green when "Spitty" up with a stone and threw it at his back. It missed John Willie and hit me instead. I had a two-inch cut on the back of my head, and "Spitty", basely given away by his "friends", was hauled in and soundly beaten.

There were no school dinners in those days, and although the dinner "hour" was usually two hours in summer quite a number of children brought sandwiches and bottles of cold tea. As some of the children came from Horsecroft, the White House (in the park), Mordebois and Martin's Green and the Monument, even the two-hour break in the summertime was hardly long enough for them to get home and back. Quite a number made the effort, though, and the Smiths from Martin's Green and the Whites from the Round House never stayed to dinner in the summer. Neither did the contingent from Little Horringer Hall. In those days it was possible to cut across the park by the paths, considerably reducing the distance. That is not possible now, as the paths have fallen into disuse and become overgrown. Anyway, there are no children to come from those places now—and if there were, transport would be provided.

The school sessions were from nine to twelve in the morning and from two till four-thirty in the afternoon in summer, with a few variations. In the winter the afternoon session was from one-thirty to four, so a considerable number of children must have often gone home in the dark. How many of today's pampered children would walk three miles across the park in the dark during the winter months? Now they have to be fetched and taken to school from St Leonard's Park—a quarter of a mile along a road lined with houses.

In the summer we played on the green, the grass being kept short by sheep grazing on it and also being cut by Mr Byford. The summers must have been drier then, for we spent hours playing fivestones, and there always seemed to be great cracks in the ground.

The day began with a few prayers led by John Willie, and a hymn. Usually one of the assistant teachers played the piano for this, though John Willie could play well. After assembly came Scripture, which lasted for about three-quarters of an hour and was always followed by arithmetic. Play was at 10.45, and lasted until eleven. There was no milk. After play came English in some form or other, composition, spelling, grammar or reading.

In the afternoon came history, geography or nature study up to playtime at three o'clock. Three afternoons a week there was, from 3.15 onwards, gardening for the senior boys with John Willie; "drawing" as it was then called for the middle and junior boys with Miss Frost or Miss Thompson, and needlework for the girls. Three solid hours a week! I seem to remember that the girls

Senior boys were instructed in gardening by Mr Curtis. In this picture, taken in 1918, the boys are Orby Ramsey, Harry Salisbury, Brian Bloomfield, Samuel Hunt, Frank Last, Samuel Herod, Sidney Sharpe, John Marriott, Percy Collins and Percy Last.

were split up, some having silent reading while the rest did needlework, and at halftime they changed round.

On Tuesdays the girls had "drawing", and on Fridays we had singing, all together under the eagle eye of John Willie. We had to stand for a full hour, and no slouching either! He was a great one for exercises and Tonic Sol-fa, and had a horrible habit of dropping on individual people and making them sing a scale or a verse to the listening, giggling audience. His favourite songs were all the patriotic ones, *Rule Britannia,* for instance, as well as *Heart of oak, Men of Harlech, The harp that once through Tara's halls, Loch Lomond, The blue bells of Scotland, Sweet and low, Early one morning,* and one I have never heard anywhere else, *Come out! 'tis now September*—he also taught the war songs, *Keep the home fires burning!* and *It's a long way to Tipperary.* For the last quarter of an hour he ran through the hymns that would be sung the next Sunday in church, and we had a few carols and Christmas hymns near Christmas.

Very often when it was too wet for gardening he would give us extra singing. At least that was a relief from needlework, and if you were lucky and could get behind one of the big boys you might be overlooked and thus avoid being dropped on to sing a scale. As most of us had the same idea, including the big boys, there was considerable jockeying for position at the beginning of the lesson. It was amazing the number of sore throats that suddenly developed when singing alone started!

Every Friday morning Lord Manners came in to take the top class for Scripture, and as he couldn't possibly teach in a room with another class we had to change over. The top class went down into the little room and Miss Coster took her class up to the far end of the big room. Lord Manners tried to make us understand, but he was far above our heads. No one played him up, for John Willie was watching, but no one learned anything either.

As far as I can remember, there was nothing very much different as Christmas approached. We had a session of carols on the last afternoon, and at the end John Willie wished us all a Happy Christmas, and hoped we would come back after the holidays "Bright and ready for work," to which sentiment we chorused the dutiful reply, "Thank you, sir, the same to you, sir!" Then we were each given an orange and a bag of sweets. I wonder who paid for them; even if oranges and sweets were cheap, to provide enough for a hundred children was no joke.

There were not half so many official visitors in those days as there are now. An inspector came about once a year, but his visit was always notified well in advance so that for some days everyone was in a flat spin. The attendance officer came more frequently, as there was a great deal of absenteeism, sometimes genuine because a child had no boots, but mostly fictitious. An older girl would be needed at home to look after the baby, so she developed a sore throat, a stomach ache or toothache. Occasionally the needlework inspectress came. Need I say more?

A frequent visitor in the old days was the school nurse, known as the "nit-nurse". Her visits were very necessary, as no school was a hundred per cent clean. Some families always had dirty heads, and the offenders were excluded until such time as their heads were clean.

There were not many breaks in the school routine during the year; in fact I can remember only two. These were the visits of the school doctor and the school dentist, whose coming caused a great upheaval as they used the small room and that meant Miss Coster's class had to move into the main room for the whole day. Pandemonium! So much coming and going, doors opening and closing, new children yelling, teachers frantic, parents conspicuous by their absence although all had been invited to come and meet the doctor.

Of course the whole hundred children did not have to be examined; only the new entrants, those who would be leaving during the year, and those who had any defect such as poor eyesight or poor hearing. There seemed to be a lot more of those than there are today.

The dentist actually paid two visits. The first time he came he examined all the children, and anyone whose teeth needed attention was given a note to take home; this had to be signed by the parents or guardian agreeing to treatment being given. Then, about a week later, the dentist came again, this time bringing a nurse with him and all his horrifying paraphernalia. Once, I remember, the nurse did not come, so poor Miss Coster had to take her place. There were usually some horrible scenes, as most children were terrified, and I do not think any anaesthetic was used. Anyway, the yells and bellows afforded entertainment to those who were lucky enough not to be on the condemned list.

John Willie had sent his own sons to the King Edward VI Grammar School in Bury, but he had no time for educated women so his daughter remained in his own school. One or two boys moved to the County Grammar School, but no girls. He was therefore outraged when my parents suggested they would like me to try for the Scholarship or Free Place to the County School, of which about ten were awarded in the area, to boys or girls. He refused point blank to give me any extra work, so on three afternoons a week I walked to Bury, where my ex-headmistress grandmother lived, and did a couple or three hours' work with her before walking home again, usually alone, as my parents could not leave the Post Office until after eight o'clock when the mail cart had gone. I was ten then, and after the house by the *Spread Eagle* there were no more, apart from Mill House, till Great Horringer Hall was reached. I did that for more than a year, and when I passed the examination John Willie took all the credit.

A word about the furniture and equipment. We were given a pen, pencil, ruler and rubber at the beginning of each day, and these were collected up at the end of the afternoon. It paid to keep on good terms with whoever was monitor for the week, as that ensured you would be given a reasonably clean pen holder and a pencil which was not too bitten at the end. The pens had wooden handles and steel nibs, and John Willie was very mean when it came to replacing broken or "crossed" nibs; it was a major operation to get a new pencil out of him—anyone would think he had to buy all the stock himself. Every exercise book was jealously guarded and grudgingly given out. The inkwells were filled on Monday mornings, and the ink was supposed to last you all the week.

We used to sit on long wooden forms, with a back rail if you were lucky. These forms were supposed to seat eight, but if the class became overcrowded ten, or even twelve, were squeezed on. Of course this led to some pushing and shoving, especially if there was a big boy at each end of the form. "A" would push everyone towards "B", who would at once push everyone back again, unless he was caught unawares and fell off the end of the form with a resounding thump, in which case "A" would lean forward interestedly and innocently, wondering how on earth that could have happened.

For lighting we had oil lamps, three in number, which were hung from chains fixed to the ceiling. It was so difficult and awkward to light these lamps that they were rarely lighted—and when they were lighted they usually smoked; anyway, they gave very little light. The only illumination we had for singing lessons in the winter was two candles on the piano.

The sanitation and washing arrangements were quite primitive. In the Infants' School there was one bucket of water drawn from the well in the middle of the school yard just outside the main door. There was a wooden cover to the well, supposed to be replaced each time a bucket of water was drawn up, but nine times out of ten it was left lying about. The bucket was raised and lowered by a rope with a hook on the end and this was wound up by an iron handle. If there was no one about it was great fun to turn the handle, then let go so the bucket rushed down into the well and the handle flew back at great speed. As far as I can remember no one ever fell in, nor was anyone hit by the flying handle.

The bucket was placed under a wooden shelf at the far end of the porch, and on the shelf were an enamel bowl and an enamel mug. There was a towel on a roller fixed on the inside of the entrance door. There was no hot water, of course.

The lavatories were outside in the playground, joined on to the coal shed. There were three lavatories, two for the girls and one for the boys, just ordinary buckets which were emptied once a week.

The water from the well varied from day to day. Sometimes it was quite clear, but after a dry spell we often found "things" in the water, usually small tadpole-like creatures, but now and again a slug or two would be drawn up. No one minded, and the water was drunk to the last drop. In the 1880s the water had been declared impure and a restriction order had been put on the well for fear of an outbreak of typhoid, diphtheria or something, but the water was still used. After all, that well was near and handy; the next well was several hundred yards away.

Things were only slightly better over at the "Big School", where water came from a pump shared by John Willie's family and the school. John Willie did not like us to use more than two pails full, and on a hot day that amount did not go far among a hundred children. There were two enamel mugs, passed from hand to hand, or rather from mouth to mouth. When I think of some of the mouths I wonder how we escaped sores and rashes and goodness knows what. There was one large roller towel for a hundred children, no soap and no warm water, though in an emergency John Willie would have some water heated in the school house.

As for the sanitation, I can only marvel that there were so few epidemics. There were two sections of the lavatory area, the girls having three cubicles, and the boys two, plus a urinal. They were bucket lavatories, emptied once a week, and by Friday they were all overflowing and the smell was appalling, especially in the summer when the stench permeated the whole school—and this situation was not remedied until the 1960s. No one who could possibly help it ever used the toilets, but even so they were woefully inadequate; as late as 1960, when I was head of the school, I was receiving notes from parents saying their children did not like using the toilets. Needless to say, there was no toilet at all for the staff.

Children who brought sandwiches for dinner were never made to wash before eating them. When I became headmistress in 1945 I insisted the children washed their hands before their meal, and so more than two buckets of water were required; but the occupant of the School House chained up the pump so that we could not get the extra pail of water we needed.

CHAPTER SIX

Curtsy to the Lady

THE ONE red letter day in the school year which we all looked forward to for many months beforehand was the school party or school treat at Ickworth, an event which was held the day after we broke up for the summer holidays.

The first party had been held about 1860 outside Ickworth Lodge, under a huge oak called the Tea Party Tree which is still standing. The location of the party was changed when the fourth Marquis of Bristol and the Marchioness moved from Ickworth Lodge into the mansion about 1907 on the death of the third marquis.

We had heard of the school treat as soon as we entered the Infants' School, and long before the time came for us to attend we knew every rule and taboo, everything that was expected of us on that greatest of days. And just to make sure that we did, just before we broke up for the summer holidays on a fine July Friday afternoon we were given a talk by Mrs Cooke on how we were to behave at the party.

Many of the children had never seen the Marquis and Marchioness of Bristol and their two daughters, Lady Marjorie and Lady Phyllis, but living in the Post Office I had seen them often. All the same, I was full of excitement as I ran across the School Yard that July afternoon, just bursting to tell anyone who would listen of the rules and intructions we had been given.

My excitement was somewhat dampened when I found that the only person with time on her hands was my headmistress grandmother, whose school in Lincolnshire must have broken up the day before we did. Anyway, she was better than nobody, so I poured out to her all the instructions we had been given by Mrs Cooke about how we were to behave from the time we started out from school to the time we arrived at Ickworth—how we were to take our mugs, to be under the beech tree on the Green at three o'clock, to be clean and tidy, to speak quietly, to keep with our partners—mine being Barbara Collins, who knew even more about the Bristols than I did, her father being their butler—not to get out of line, and not to walk in the cowpats, of which there were plenty in the park, and so on and so forth.

"We go along Geraldine's Walk," I said "and Lord and Lady Bristol will be waiting for us on the lawn, and we all go up to

The Tea Party Tree near Ickworth Lodge under which the school treats were held for nearly half a century. Ickworth Lodge can be seen in the background.

them, and say 'good afternoon,' and the boys bow, and the girls curtsy..."

I was not prepared for the explosion caused by that simple remark. My grandmother swelled to twice her normal size, her usually pale face turned purple, and she hissed, "You will do no such thing! No grandchild of mine shall curtsy to anybody. You are as good as they are—and if I hear you have curtsied—I'll floor you!" (That was a favourite threat of hers.)

She kept on and on at me until at last, utterly bewildered, I disengaged myself from her clutching hand and fled to my favourite sanctuary in one of the empty pig sties. I knew she would never follow me there, as she objected so strongly to my father "lowering himself" by keeping pigs.

I simply did not understand it. I knew some of the children and women "bobbed a curtsy" whenever they saw one of the Family, and the men took off their caps—and no one thought anything of it. What I did not realise was that while Horringer was still strongly feudal my grandmother had spent many years in the Midlands, where feudalism was dead. On the other hand, she should have been the first to realise that if a rule had been made by the school authorities, in this case John Willie, that rule should be kept. Looking back, I wish I had been old and bold enough to ask her what she would do if a child was encouraged by its parents, or grandparents as in my case, to break one of the rules she had made for her school. She would have "floored them," I expect.

To return to the pigsty. I just did not understand what the fuss was all about—how could I be as good as Lady Bristol, or Lady Marjorie or Lady Phyllis? They lived in the mansion, didn't they? Of one thing I was quite sure, on no account was I going to miss the party. But what a dilemma faced me! Not to curtsy would incur the wrath of Mrs Cooke and John Willie; to do so would mean that my life would be a misery for the rest of my grandmother's stay, and for all the other holidays when she came to Horringer—like an elephant she would never forget, nor forgive.

At last I slunk out of the sty and scuttled up the road to my friend Barbara Collins. She was not much help; she didn't see that it mattered, but then she hadn't got a grandmother staying with her, and she wasn't in danger of being "floored". However, she did hatch up a plan of a sort; she and I would walk at the end of the crocodile, and may be something would turn up before we came face to face with the Bristols.

So I went home, smelling of pig, I suppose, to find the atmosphere somewhat strained. My father had basely deserted my mother and filled the office with half a dozen cronies; my mother, who was scared stiff of my grandmother, had gone to see the Salvages; my sister had gone to bed, and I bided my time until my grandmother went for her usual evening walk (she went every evening as the smell of the hot sealing wax got on her chest) and then joined my sister in the bedroom.

I have no recollection of the next morning. All I can remember is that in the early afternoon I was arrayed in my best frock—white muslin—my hair was brushed, for hours it seemed, I was given a mug, and with admonitions to "behave like a little lady—and don't let me hear you have curtsied" off I went to the rendezvous under the beech tree, where I joined up with Barbara. While the infants gathered under the tree the contingent from the Big School assembled in the playground.

Although we children were thrilled at the thought of the party, the teachers were not so enamoured of the idea. For one thing it meant giving up a Saturday afternoon, and for another it meant a journey up from Bury for Miss Frost. John Willie and Mrs Cooke suffered the most as instead of being themselves they put on what they thought were genteel voices, praying all the while that no catastrophe would happen. Teacher Flo, in the whitest, starchiest white pinafore, prayed that no one would notice her.

Barbara and I managed to stay at the end of the queue, much to the surprise of Teacher Flo, who knew from experience that we were not in the habit of hiding our lights under bushels. I expect she put it down to first-party nerves, always thinking the best of her charges. The crocodile ambled across the park, taking the path which led to the stables, John Willie and Miss Frost keeping the hundred or so children from the Big School in some sort of order while Mrs Cooke and Teacher Flo looked after the thirty-six infants, picking up mugs (mostly enamel or tin), wiping noses (Teacher Flo's job, needless to say), exhorting various infants overcome by excitement to "Go behind that tree over there" and so on. The sight of Iris Cooke cheered me immensely; surely if she could curtsy, her father being a builder and a sidesman in church, so could I!

We filed through the kissing gate with a good deal of pushing and shoving, walked sedately along the moss-covered Geraldine's Walk, and the North Lawn was in front of us, looking like lovely green velvet. At the sight of the head of the crocodile emerging

from the trees the small group of people awaiting our arrival came towards us. A few seconds more and it would be over . . .

But something was the matter. John Willie was talking to Lady Bristol. Then he turned to the waiting crowd of children: "Her Ladyship thinks it would save a lot of time if you said 'Good afternoon' all together."

Talk about relief! Everyone bellowed "Good afternoon, your Ladyship" and "Good afternoon, your Lordship" and, at a signal from John Willie and with a yell of excitement, we all broke ranks and raced off to our various plays. The big boys raced across to the cricket pitch on the North Lawn, the younger children made for the two seesaws, the swing and the wooden roundabout. John Willie and Mrs Cooke stood talking to Lord and Lady Bristol, while Miss Coster, Miss Frost and Teacher Flo supervised the rest of us.

Long tables were set up under the trees and the staff were busy setting out the tea—mountains of bread and butter, slices of fruit cake, and plates of iced Genoese sponge, cut into small pieces. The latter were very popular and much sought after; needless to say we little ones never had a piece!

After tea we formed up into a crocodile again, big ones first, and filed into the Rotunda, where there were tables covered with presents. Each child received a present—books, knives, balls,

In the photograph on the opposite page of the school treat of 1911 Lady Bristol is wearing the robes she had worn at the Coronation of King George V. Talking to her is Lady Phyllis, and Lord Bristol is behind her with his aunt, Lady Mary. On the right the pupils are sitting down at the tables laid out on the lawn.

dolls, trumpets, drums, doll's tea sets, the choice seemed endless. I had a coloured rubber ball, I remember.

John Willie thanked our hosts, we gave three cheers, and the party was over for another year. All Horringer knew when we were on our way home by the blaring of toy trumpets, the banging of drums and the squabbles and scuffles that broke out on the way back. Miss Coster had slipped away down to the gardens, Mrs Cooke and Iris had taken the short cut through the wood, Miss Frost and Teacher Flo ambled along, picking up lost handkerchiefs and hair ribbons, and John Willie stalked along in splendid isolation.

That party was the highlight of the school's year for something like a century, being dropped in 1976. Rather a pity, but times have changed, and so have the children.

I do not remember ever being asked by my grandmother about the curtsying, and I never found out why it was dropped. No one was ever again expected to curtsy at the party, but I shall never forget my feelings the night before my first party when I was between the devil and the deep blue sea.

A herd of deer in Ickworth Park.

CHAPTER SEVEN

The Park

WE ALL loved the park. Winter and summer, it was always there; it became part of us, and we took its permanence for granted. We played in it, we walked in it, we knew every inch of it, and we knew all its moods. After playing in the park every spare moment during the week, we were taken for a walk in it every Sunday.

There were very few rules concerning the park, and we respected the few there were. The first rule was on a wooden noticeboard fastened to one of the sweet chestnut trees just inside the park; it said simply "No dogs allowed in the park." We kept that rule—the local dogs were never taken inside the park gates. The only other rule that I can remember is that the woods were private and only the gamekeepers and woodmen were allowed in them. I have lived near Adkin's Wood all my life and I have never walked the entire length of it. The millions of rabbits in the park, helped by the sheep, kept the grass short, the entire acreage looking like a vast lawn criss-crossed by various paths which led to the mansion via the stables on the left-hand side of the road; to Ickworth Lodge, to Mordebois Cottage and Little Horringer Hall and Slough Lane; and sharp right, to Briar Cottage. Those paths were in what was called Horringer Park (although as children we did not know it, the boundary between Horringer and Ickworth went across the park, crossing the present cricket and football pitches, so really the name Horringer Park was correct).

Beyond Ickworth House was the Deer Park, and here paths led to the gardens, to the White House, round beside the lake to the small Round House, up to Martin's Green and the Monument; back to the small Round House, past Fairy Lake, turning sharp right at the entrance to the Mowing Ground, through Brick Kiln meadow, Bilson's meadow and so out on to the main road at the top end of the village.

Our favourite playground was just inside the park, on both sides of the drive. There were two ponds on each side, all rather smelly and never cleaned out. The one we liked best was the one on the left of the path, half way towards the stables. It was the smelliest, of course, but here the best "creatures" could be found, especially water snails. The times we fell in that pond and had to run home, covered in mud and debris and stinking! In the summer we would dry our wet garments in the sun, hanging them on a bush or on the lower boughs of a tree.

The ponds on the right and left just inside the park were never very popular with us for some reason. They were usually choked with dead leaves. On the other hand we spent hours playing along the Dairy Ditch, which was narrow enough to be jumped and wide enough for paddling. Bits of stick could be floated under the bridges which carried the path to Ickworth Lodge and the one towards Mordebois and Saxham.

Unfortunately there were holes in the banks of the Dairy Ditch, and these holes were in great demand by wasps which made their nests there. Many of us had at one time or another inadvertently jumped into a wasps' nest and fled yelling towards the Park gates in search of the bluebag, that washday accessory so soothing when rubbed on a wasp sting.

We played every game imaginable. The paths were bare and made good cricket pitches, and the grass was short enough to allow us to play our everlasting game of fivestones.

Often we went deeper into the park, down to the lake by the kitchen gardens for instance. On the way we passed Parson's Pond, so called because until the early eighteenth century it had been in the garden of the Ickworth Parsonage. The Parsonage was demolished in the eighteenth century and the bricks used to build Chedburgh Rectory. It is quite an attractive pond, with its weeping willow tree, but we did not like it because it was where the men who worked in the park drowned unwanted cats and kittens, and it was said that the mewing of ghostly cats could be heard on certain nights. At the lake our most popular game was paddling in the brook which flowed into the lake or sliding down the concrete ramp, sometimes on purpose, sometimes accidentally.

There were times when we moved across towards the White House and played in the great stretches of bracken, very often disturbing a deer with her fawn, or startling the whole herd of deer. We were used to seeing the Shetland ponies; one kept clear of them because the older ones were inclined to bite.

Sometimes we went to the Fairy Lake, a lovely spot, and looked speculatively at the rotten punt in the old boathouse, wondering if we dare risk trying a trip across the lake. We never did.

For several years some of us, half a dozen or so, had to journey across the park before school to fetch the milk from the dairy. We took tin milk cans with us, though I remember the Collins children had a white enamel can which was greatly envied. Some from large families took two cans. Skimmed milk was ha'penny a pint; unskimmed, a penny a pint. Winter and summer, rain or shine, we went across to the dairy in the early morning,

The kitchen gardens of Ickworth seen across the lake.

three-hundred-and-sixty-five days a year. We rarely hurried, even in the winter; actually we dawdled, as it was only half a mile across the grass.

We had a game we used to play on the way home, sometimes with unfortunate consequences! This was to swing the can, full of milk, in a circle round your head. There was a knack to it, just the slightest hesitation and the lid would come off and the unfortunate "swinger" would be deluged in milk. That was very funny to the onlookers, who had probably caused the "swinger" to hesitate by making her laugh, but it was not so funny for the victim, who not only had to go home to be wiped down but had to make a second trip over to the dairy, usually alone, with one of her own ha'pennies or pennies to get another pint of milk. It sometimes meant missing breakfast, too. Some people were good at swinging; I never saw Barbara Collins lose a drop of milk. I must have been easily amused, I lost gallons! Perhaps her can-lid fitted better than mine did.

The park was useful in other ways. At a time when every penny counted, to get something for nothing except a little effort was of paramount importance. An all-the-year-round pastime was sticking, done mostly by the women in the afternoons, by the children as soon as school was over, and by the men on their way home from work. As everyone had coal fires sticks were a necessity; it was impossible to light the fire without them.

But the most important way of making a little extra money was acorning, many of the village people relying on the money they

earned from picking up acorns to pay their rent. I was always led
to believe (in those days) that a surfeit of acorns was dangerous to
cattle, so they were collected, stored in the shed which was used
(and still is) as a cricket pavilion in summer, and doled out to the
animals in small quantities during the winter.

Acorning started towards the end of October, picking being
done chiefly by women and children. The women went in the
afternoons when their household chores were finished and the
children went before school, in the dinner hour and after school.
Some people went as soon as it was light in the morning and
stayed all day, taking bread and cheese and cold tea, and picked
up until it was too dark to see the acorns. There were favourite
trees which always bore big acorns, and there was great
competition to stake a claim to one of those.

Most women took kneelers with them, rather like thin has-
socks, as after some hours on the knees without a kneeler, the
skin would be broken, and the knee would fester.

The acorns would be picked up into a small container, a tin, a

The Fairy Lake, a lovely spot where the children thought of risking a trip in a
leaky punt, but never did.

milk can or a saucepan with a hole in it, and this receptacle was emptied into a box or basket, which was in turn emptied into a sack. An old pram or a box on wheels provided the ideal means of bringing the acorns home.

When the season opened the head forester, Mr John Curtis, would put a notice up on the barn doors which served in those days as the village notice board stating the price per bushel which would be paid, and the day acorns would be collected from the cottages. The price varied from fourpence a bushel in a year when acorns were plentiful, to the enormous price of half-a-crown a bushel paid one glorious year. As rents were about a shilling a week, the amount needed was soon earned.

At the end of the season men came round with a waggon and a bushel measure and weighed out the acorns. On a set day the head forester would meet all the collectors, usually in his office, to pay them for their labours. Some people collected forty bushels or more; I remember I once collected ONE bushel.

Blackberrying was an enjoyable pastime. There were some very good bushes in the park, down Jarvises and along the Sunken Walk, and these were soon stripped by the women and children.

There were one or two crab apple trees, and these were in great demand among those who liked blackberry and apple jelly. These trees seem to have disappeared; so does the cherry apple tree near the boundary of the cricket ground.

Mushrooming was not very popular with us, as it meant getting up early in the morning to go collecting. The best mushrooms were found on Icehouse Hill, though a few grew beside the paths. Workmen on their way home to breakfast would sometimes bring in the large coarse mushrooms which grew under the trees. Often a foot or more in diameter, these were known as "horse" mushrooms and while not popular for eating were used extensively for making ketchup.

Then there were the nut trees, not just the hazel nut stubs which were found in many places, but also walnuts and sweet chestnuts. We did not have to go far to find the sweet chestnuts, as there are still two large sweet chesnut trees just inside the park on the left-hand side of the drive, but to find walnuts we had to go right down to the Deer Park, where there are trees opposite Ickworth Church; there was not much point in going all that way as the children from the gardens, White House and stables had probably been there before us, and in any case there were walnut trees in the village, three of them in our orchard.

If there was enough snow in the winter we would trudge across to Icehouse Hill with our sledges and have a marvellous time. Occasionally, too, there would be skating on the lake, but the frosts were not very often sharp enough for that.

The Icehouse itself held a great attraction for us. To begin with, it was rather difficult to get into; the climb down usually ended in a slither, and when you arrived at the bottom there was really nothing to see, just a rotting wooden door to an underground chamber, small, dank and dark. It is a wonder we did not break our limbs climbing up and down into the pit, but apart from a few bruises or grazes we survived.

The Busted Canal Bank was another favourite place for our games. When there was any water in the stream—or, to give it its proper name, the River Linnet—we used to paddle there.

As children we gave no thought to the origin of the Busted Canal Bank, but later in life I learnt that it had an interesting story connected with the diversion of a road that until 1814 ran from Bury to Chevington. In bygone ages that road must have been used by abbots and other important folk, but when in 1808 the Little Saxham estate was added to the Horringer estate the fifth Earl of Bristol, later the first marquis, found himself with this public road running right across his private land. He persuaded Parliament to allow him to close the old road on condition that he built another road through Little Saxham and Chevington to take its place. He had a new road, the present one between Bury and Chevington, constructed at a cost of £2,000, a great sum for those days, and spent nearly as much in having another road made to Chedburgh and Rede.

That was all very well, but the Old "Cheventon Way" was shorter and people did not like the changes, so they continued to use the old road in spite of orders, notices and goodness knows what. Something had to be done about it, so the Earl announced that he was going to have an ornamental lake covering fifteen acres constructed right across the line of the old road. This was quite feasible, for other lakes had already been made in the park as part of earlier landscaping schemes. In 1823 a high dam was thrown up across the Chevington Way and the water covered the road, but the Earl's triumph was short-lived. Some time after 1842, owing to some fault in its construction the dam burst and the waters poured down to Bury, flooding the area round the *Spread Eagle*. The dam had cost £500 to construct, and now all the money was wasted; everyone said it served the Earl right, and that the bursting of the dam was an Act of God.

We didn't know all this; we just knew that the Busted Canal Bank was a fine place to play. It was a long way to go, but worth it!

There were two or three trees in the park that we liked. There was the huge oak by Ickworth Lodge known as the "Tea Party Tree" because that was where the first school treats were held, and there was "Lord Bristol's walking stick"—I don't know which

Lord Bristol—another oak tree which we passed every day on our way to and from the dairy. Also near the dairy path was a group of lime trees which we loved to stand under and sniff, listening to the bees having a marvellous time among the lime flowers.

There was a story about another oak tree in the same area that during the wars with France the Commissioners of the Admiralty came round looking for suitable trees to build the "wooden-walls" necessary for our defence. They inspected the trees in the park and decided this particular oak was on its last legs and would not last more than a year or so, and they declined to take it; that was in 1793—the tree is still there, hale and hearty.

The "Double Oaks" are, as the name implies, two oak trees on the right-hand side of the drive, at the top of the hill. "I went as far as the Double Oaks" or "Don't go beyond the Double Oaks" were well-known expressions.

Another tree that intrigued us very much was a large oak tree on the other side of the drive, just beyond the "Double Oaks", with a large area of the trunk painted bright green. The paint covered up the scar where a bough had come off, and we were told it was there to prevent the ponies and horses being frightened by the light expanse of new wood. There may have been some truth in that, but really I think the painting was done to preserve the tree; no other tree was ever treated like that in the park.

Then there was the "goss", an area of nettles and brambles and young trees with a path through it, all carefully wired in with two gates in the wire. I have never been able to find out why that particular area was wired in, unless it was something to do with the pheasants. It was never called the "gorse" but always the "goss"—and I know now that "goss" was used for "gorse" by Shakespeare.

CHAPTER EIGHT

Those Special Days

VERY FEW of the ordinary people had a settled holiday each
year, as there was no such thing as holidays with pay. If a
man was away from work for a few days, or even for one day, for
whatever reason, he lost his pay. However, we did have one or two
special days in Horringer, and the one that was looked forward to
by all was Whit Monday.

It was THE red letter day for the whole village, and the
Almighty must have been inundated with prayers from Horringer
people that it would be fine. All the females in the village
reckoned to have a new frock for that day, which was also the
West Suffolk Friendly Society's Club Day.

Horringer Brass Band had rehearsed for weeks beforehand,
usually practising on the piece of grass behind the Men's Club
(now "Highlands"). Living next door, as you might say, we at the
Post Office were very glad when Whit Monday was over for the
year. Early in the morning of Whit Monday the members of the
band would call at the Institute to collect their instruments, their
banner and other impedimenta, which were always kept in the
library, then off they went up to Sharpe's Lane corner, followed by
every child in the village. Here they formed a procession, after a
lot of fussing and any number of false starts. Bill Rowe was the
most important figure—he beat the bass drum.

At last they all got going and set off down the street, blowing
and banging for all they were worth. The banner, of deep blue silk
with the words "West Suffolk Friendly Society" appliquéed on it in
gold braid, and with a fringe of gold all round it, was carried in
front, billowing out like the sail of a great ship. The banner was
followed by Bill Rowe, beating the big drum as though his life
depended on it. All the children of the village followed behind the
band, as well as many of the not-so-young, all skipping, hopping
and jumping in the sunshine.

As far as I can remember the band knew only one tune,
Onward, Christian Soldiers, which they played with gusto.

At the church gate the procession was met by the parson, in the
same position as he met a coffin at a funeral. The choir were also
waiting, and when the procession arrived everyone sang *Onward,*

The scene of festivity, the cricket ground in the
park, as it is today.

Christian Soldiers; some of the choir boys must have done a quick change, as a couple of minutes before they had been following the big drum. After that the parson and choir led the way into church, followed by the procession, drum and all, for a short service, with only one hymn—need I say it, *Onward, Christian Soldiers.*

After the service everyone came out of church and the band and procession went all round the village, the band stopping to play its one tune outside every house where the bandsmen thought they might be given refreshment. Then, tired by this perambulation, the bandsmen and the club men went down to the school for a "dinner"—there was no village hall or community centre then— and everyone else rushed home and swallowed their meal, grudging every moment spent away from the excitement. Then we all went to the school to wait until the men came out, and it seemed a very long wait.

About three o'clock, while they could still walk, the men came out and staggered across the park to the cricket pitch, still clinging to their instruments. Every now and then a few ragged bars of what was apparently meant to be *Onward, Christian Soldiers* was wafted across the grass.

In a tent erected on the cricket ground you could get beer or a

The Horringer and Ickworth Brass Band in their smart uniforms.

full tea for three pence, sausage rolls and all. All the afternoon there were sports for everyone, and now and again a verse of *O.C.S.*—though that became more and more wobbly as time went on. Old Mrs Parker, who kept the shop, had a stall in the acorn shed—I beg its pardon, the cricket pavilion—and there you could buy a sausage roll and a glass of ginger pop for a penny.

In the evening everyone trailed back to the village. The band went in front, of course, with only the big drum still banging. Not that the festivities were yet over.

A marquee had been put up on the green and in this a dance was held. The grass was usually rather high, as Whit Monday was always in late May or early June, but no one minded. Everyone was there, from babies in arms to old people, who on other days were bed-ridden, and for music they had Bill Foster and his concertina, and sometimes a fiddle as well. The parson always gave a barrel of lemon squash, for the dancers became very hot, what with the long grass and everything. That was for the women and children; the men had a barrel of beer.

When the men were all drunk and the women exhausted, everyone went home to bed. And that was that for another year.

The other important holiday in the life of the village was and still is the day of the flower show, though this is not as exciting as it used to be. The flower show was first held in Horringer in 1886, though it had been suggested by Mr Heigham, the rector, four years earlier. We know that the show was definitely in being by 1886 because Mr Giddens, who was rector then, wrote to the estate agent on 16th September, 1886, "Of course you know the Flower Show is tomorrow."

At one time the flower show was held down the road in Byford's Meadow, the meadow behind the present garage. Later on it was held in Cook's Meadow, the one between The Knoll and Street Farm, and then for many years it was held in the meadow behind the Institute. A marquee was set up until 1919 when the old village hall was given to the village by the fourth Marchioness of Bristol, after which the marquee was no longer required.

Many of the exhibits were brought in overnight, just as they are now, and often there were allegations that vegetables had been "changed", especially if the favourite did not win his usual prizes. Later, the caretaker of the Institute sat up all night in order to prevent any nefarious goings-on. There was no flower show committee, the show being run by the Men's Club.

The classes were much as they are today, especially those for fruit and vegetables, but the needlework classes have changed— there is no longer a class for "Plain Shirt, man's, with a gusset." The schoolchildren used to put in writing, drawing, needlework (aprons made of stiff calico, with gathers), knitted vests and plain socks. There was also a prize for the best "specimen", which consisted of a six-inch square of white calico showing every conceivable sewing stitch (I never got beyond hemming round the edge of mine, and even at that stage it was certainly far from white, being pale brown with red spots—marks of honest toil). The children also collected wild flowers. For women there were prizes for the best cake, loaf and eggs, and there were classes for jam and bottled fruit, and later on, home-made wine.

For the exhibitors, the show was the big attraction. For the rest of us, the huge majority, the Men's Club hired Crichton's fair. It used to arrive the day before the show, a number of horse-drawn caravans and a steam engine to drive the roundabouts, and we used to sit on the wall of one of the pigsties to watch the caravans drive in. My father, whose orchard adjoined the meadow where the fair was held, was about the only person in the village who thought Lady Bristol had the right idea in banning the fair, but then he lost several good chickens each time the fair came.

There was a big roundabout with gaily painted horses; swing boats, shooting galleries, and all kinds of sideshows and stalls. The first stall, kept by the filthiest old woman I had ever seen, sold rock, and we were strictly forbidden to buy any. It was said that she made her rock by spitting on her hands and rolling sugar in the saliva; the brown colour of the rock came from the dirt on her hands. Needless to say, our first port of call was the rock stall! There were also ice-creams, which we bought. How we avoided food poisoning, I do not know, but it was all fun, what with the fairy lights and the roundabout organ grinding out all the latest song hits.

About six o'clock the prizes for the vegetables and so on were presented to the winners by Lady Bristol, and a little later the tent was cleared of all exhibits. The fair had to close by ten, but we had gone home to bed long before that; it was part of the enjoyment of the day to lie in bed and listen to the music and watch the twinkling of the lights until the fair closed down.

Of course the 1914-18 war put an end to all this. An attempt was made to revive the fair when the war was over, but somehow it wasn't the same and a lot of the glamour was lost. The fair people themselves seemed rougher each year, and some of the more "genteel" people in the village grumbled about them; the rector, Lord Manners, wanted the fair moved further away from the Rectory grounds, though the committee would not agree to a move. The end came one year when it rained all day on flower show day; the fair people did not take enough money to make the thing pay, then the traction engine got stuck in the mud and they spent half a day trying to get it out. The language used by the fair people that day was "something awful"—and who should come by

The Horringer and Ickworth Institute, formerly the Rectory and now known as Highlands. It ceased to house the rector about 1850 and was turned into the Institute in 1876, continuing as such until the new Community Centre was built.

at a crucial moment but Lady Bristol. Before long the committee had a letter of complaint from her, and the fair was never asked to come to Horringer again. Since then the flower shows have been models of respectability—but we still remember with pleasure the anticipation and the fun of those years long ago when the lights and the music added an extra dimension to village life.

There were one or two other "special days", but they were not looked forward to very much by the children because we youngsters were more or less forced into taking part. One of these special occasions was the annual concert, arranged by some well-meaning ladies of the village in aid of some good cause, missionaries or something like that. Of course we children did not know what went on behind the scenes before and after the performance, but I know now that all was not sweetness and light; far from it!

As all the functions organised in the village came under the umbrella of the Men's Institute, and as my father was secretary of that august body for many years, we always knew before the other children when a function was pending. It was therefore no surprise to my sister and me when some morning John Willie stumped into school, snapped at Miss Coster, who played the hymn at morning assembly, raised his eyes to heaven as if to implore the Almighty to give him strength, gabbled a couple of prayers, then, trying to put a brave face on it, said "There is going to be a concert on 19th December, organised by some ladies in the village, and they have very kindly suggested that you children should take part in the programme. It is a very great honour for us to be asked to appear in the programme, so we must all do our best to make the concert a success. I shall discuss with the teachers what we can do."

His remarks were received with no overwhelming show of enthusiasm, I must say. It meant rehearsing after school, usually in classrooms that had become very cold as the fires had gone out by then. After school *was* after school, so discipline was not so strict—and John Willie was obviously not a hundred per cent in favour of the idea. Besides, we were rather limited in our choice of items. The "gentry" put on a sort of pantomime, and we did not see any of that until the night of the dress rehearsal; the glee club (the forerunner of the Horringer Singers) did most of their rehearsing at the Rectory, supervised by Lord Manners; and we fitted in wherever there was a gap in the programme.

The concert took place on a Saturday evening. With hindsight, I cannot for the life of me see how it ever got off the ground. The stage had been put up between the end of school and the time of the dress rehearsal on Friday by the estate carpenters and workmen; scenery had been brought over in the market cart; and pot plants came on the Saturday morning, grudgingly loaned by Mr Coster, the head gardener. I think the participants in the play came dressed for action, as there was nowhere to change. Older members of the Men's Club who were not in the glee club were "on the door" or ushered members of the audience to their seats. Chairs had been brought over from the Rectory for those wealthy people who had bought two-shilling tickets; the holders of one-shilling tickets sat on school forms with backs, while the sixpenny ticket holders sat on the older backless forms at the back of the room or stood along the sides.

One memorable year it was decided that the schoolchildren should do maypole dancing. Whoever thought of that idea must have been completely nuts. Maypole dancing on firm ground with plenty of elbow-room is bad enough, but maypole dancing on a small, shaky stage is next to impossible, especially as the boys loathed the whole thing and considered having to dance with a "lot of old gals" a tremendous indignity. There was no such thing as gym shoes; we all danced in our ordinary shoes, or in the case of some of the boys in hob-nailed boots. We had been threatened with death and destruction if we let go of our ribbons, and had been told not to sway the maypole.

All went well to begin with. Then, for some reason, the music quickened. Round and round we went, faster and faster—thump, thump, thump, went the boys. Then the inevitable happened: the maypole started to sway, Barbara Collins missed her footing and, still clinging to her ribbon, she flew off the stage into the front row of the audience and landed in Lord Bristol's lap! The maypole went over, the rest of us tangled in the ribbons. The boys, who I am sure had engineered the whole thing, bellowed with laughter, and Barbara, becoming aware of her august resting place, yelled blue murder.

Calm was eventually restored, and as the school had broken up for Christmas we hoped John Willie would have forgotten the incident by the time we went back to school in January. But John Willie must have been an elephant in a previous existence; he never forgot, and those responsible for the debacle were speedily dealt with.

One year it was decided in place of the Christmas concert to hold a fete at Ickworth, not on the North Lawn where we had the annual school treat but on the South Lawn. Teas were on sale in the Orangery and stalls were set up on the lawn. Instead of the usual play the "gentry" performed an item called "Living Whist," which was very good, I thought. It did not last very long, and as most of the ordinary men and women could play whist they could follow the game.

Each child had a large cardboard card tied round his or her waist, each card representing a playing card. The smaller children wore the less important cards; mine was the three of clubs, I remember. Four adults stood on boxes at the four points of the compass. When the pianist started to play, the children formed a large ring and danced round, dropping off one at a time in front of the adults. That was quite easy, unless you missed your adult and threw everyone out. When all the "cards" were dealt, the game proceeded like an ordinary game of whist—each of the adults called the card he or she was playing, and when our card was called we just skipped into the middle with three other cards, and then skipped off to stand behind whichever one of the adults had won the trick. I can't remember if we played more than one hand, but I can remember all the girls wore white dresses, the sun shone, and there was a good crowd; I wonder why it was never repeated?

Although we lost several of our special days owing to the Great War, that did lead to the introduction of a new one, Armistice Sunday. I can remember the first Remembrance Sunday. By November, 1919, all the men who had survived the slaughter had been demobilised and were home again, my father being one of the last to return. He arrived in September, 1919, having had a long way to come from Salonika. When it was given out that there would be a Remembrance Service on the second Sunday in November and that it was going to be a special service with a bugler to sound *Last Post* rumours abounded as to what really was going to happen at the service; I remember the thrill of excitement that swept through us all when one of the bigger boys told us "You want to come to church on Sunday night, 'Slosher' Smith is going to blow the 'Cookhouse'."

Armistice (or "Armistick" as the old folks pronounced it) Sunday has been celebrated ever since, but "Slosher" Smith performed only once.

There was one other special day, but it was only "special" for a very few people. This was the dinner given at the *Six Bells* and later at the Institute on every New Year's Day for "six worthy widows." The dinner was cooked on the premises, and the main course consisted of a huge steak and kidney pudding. The only man allowed to attend the dinner was the rector, Lord Manners Hervey, who manfully went along year after year. The main object of one of the widows, a gay old spark if ever there was one, was to kiss Lord Manners under the mistletoe; as he was a lean six foot two and she a tubby five foot nothing I don't think she ever achieved her ambition. This dinner died out about 1945.

The *Six Bells* looks quite a modern house but is probably built on old foundations; it was a farmhouse before becoming a public house.

CHAPTER NINE

Fun and Games

LOOKING BACK nostalgically at my Horringer childhood, it seems to me that we spent most of our time at play. Perhaps we did, perhaps we did not, but the games we played were important to us.

Most of the games we played were seasonal, and the apparatus we used was home-made or cost a very few pence. Our chief playground was the park, though there were times when we played on the main road. Looking at that road with the continual stream of traffic passing along it today, it is difficult to realise that sixty years ago that same road would have been filled with boys and girls playing with their tops or hoops.

There were two kinds of tops, both made of wood and crudely painted, a short stumpy one known as a Tubs and one with a longer shank, known as a Lanky. The Tubs cost a penny at Parker's shop, and the Lanky cost twopence. Its extra cost made the Lanky a status symbol. It didn't matter if you could spin it or not, if you owned a Lanky you were somebody. Not many children had twopence to spend casually—we only had a penny a week. The whips we used were usually an ordinary stick with a groove about an inch from the top which held the piece of thick string or cord. A thin piece of leather such as a leather bootlace was much coveted, and so was a piece of garden cane in place of an ordinary piece of stick—cane was apt to splinter, but it did last longer than an ordinary stick. Of course, it was tempting to go for the legs and not for the top, especially if the legs belonged to someone you didn't like. We played with these tops for hours on end, and were only interrupted by a tumbril, a pony trap or a ridden horse; no one would dream of hitting a top at a horse.

Hoops came out every spring. The boys usually had iron ones and the girls had wooden ones, plain unvarnished wood and not painted as hoops are today. I don't know where the iron hoops came from, or the iron "sticks", but I seem to remember hearing that blacksmiths could be persuaded to make the iron hoops. Sometimes the boys used an iron hoop from a cask—but these were only used as a last resort.

As soon as the ground was dry enough the boys started to play cricket on the green or along one of the paths in the park. The wickets they used were sticks sharpened at one end, extremely irregular in shape. The bats were home-made and liable to split at any minute, and the balls varied from ordinary rubber balls to discarded tennis balls. Although this equipment was very primitive, Horringer turned out some excellent cricketers.

Football was not very popular when I was young, but its popularity increased among the boys as their fathers and elder brothers became interested in the game.

The most popular summer game was fivestones, both boys and girls spending many hours playing this. We must have had very dry summers then, for I remember that it was quite a common occurrence for a "stone" to go into a crack in the earth—and if the summer had been wet we could not have sat on the grass for such long periods without developing pneumonia! Fivestones, which was the forerunner of the modern game of "Jacks", was a very complicated game and varied from district to district. In Horringer the game was divided into two main sections, called "Horringer" and "Bury"; there was also a third part, but I don't know much about that one, never having reached so far. It is very difficult to find anyone now who can remember all the sections of the game.

Although called fivestones, it was usually played with marbles, the same glass marbles or alleys which were used as stoppers in ginger beer bottles. As time went on these plain glass marbles were replaced by coloured glass ones costing a farthing each which could be bought in the shop. Again, not many children

When Zoë Leech was growing up in Horringer the Street was quiet enough to serve as a playground. The solitary car in this picture was the precursor of hordes.

could afford to buy marbles, but again marbles were a status symbol—the poorer children used ordinary stones, those not quite so poor used plain glass marbles, while those who had more money to spend had coloured glass marbles.

There were advantages and disadvantages in playing with the glass alleys. While they were uniform in size and shape, the alleys were more difficult to pick up and rolled more easily, which was not so good in those parts of the game when the "stones" were not supposed to touch each other. Besides, they were rather large for small hands to hold.

"Horringer" was the easy part of the game. For the first item, the five "stones" were tossed on to the back of the hand, and those which stayed on were then tossed back into the palm. If no "stones" stayed on the back of the hand you were "out" right away and had to wait for the next turn round.

Having successfully caught at least one "stone", in your palm, you then proceeded to pick up the others, one at a time; you threw up one "stone", picked up one "marble stone" and then caught the one you had thrown up as it came down. You were allowed to move the "stones" into more favourable positions; for instance, if one was caught in a tuft of grass you were allowed to move it to a smoother spot.

If you succeeded in picking up all the "stones" you then went on to the next stage, in which these had to be picked up two at a time. Failure to pick up any "stone" meant you were "out". Then to three together, then to four at once.

The next part of the game was called "scramblers". In this the "stones" were thrown down, one was picked up to act as the one to be thrown up, and then all the rest had to be picked up in one fell swoop, which required quite a knack.

Then came "Piccadilly", which was easy. The "stones" were turned on to the back of the hand, and then into the palm. Those "stones" which were caught were held in the palm, the others being picked up one at a time. After that was "Puzzles", and this was harder. The "stones" were tossed as usual, then all those caught in the palm were thrown up at once, and all the others picked up one at a time. "Jinks" was next, and in this those not caught in the palm had to be picked up and clinked together; no clink and you were "out".

"No Jinks" which came next meant that those "stones" which were not caught had to be picked up without clinking together. That finished "Horringer", and if anyone ever got as far, "Bury" came next.

The routine for "Bury" was the same, but the beginnings were different. The "stones" were not turned on to the back of the hand but were scattered. If two "stones" touched, you were "out", so the "stones" had to be thrown fairly wide apart. That is where the disadvantage of playing with marbles came in; they seemed to gravitate towards each other.

Another very popular pastime was dressing up, and for that tablecloths and old curtains were in great demand. We used to act plays and charades down in our orchard, while we played all sorts of games "down the park"—nothing organised, just whatever we thought we would play. We had our own "friends" or "familiars", too. Wake Collins had a special "friend" who lived in the corner of the meadow bordering the Lower Way—actually in the corner of Cater's garden; this "friend" was called King Catalini—goodness knows where he found that name!

Of course, when the boys played cricket along the worn paths in the park the girls were not allowed to play with them. There was no such thing as Women's Lib in those days.

Very few children had any elaborate toys, and apart from a few of the lucky ones our toys were either home-made or bought for a penny or two at one of the village jumble sales, though it was considered extravagant, even shiftless, to spend money on toys, however cheap they were.

Most of the girls had a doll of some sort. The majority were rag dolls which could be made at home and dressed in scraps left over from the home-made dresses the girls wore themselves. Now and again a Dutch doll was still to be seen, hard, uncomfortable to nurse, brightly painted, though the paint was liable to run if the doll was left out in the rain. I can remember part of a poem concerning such a catastrophe—it went rather like this:

> I once had a dear little doll, dear,
> The most beautiful doll in the world.
> Her cheeks were so red and so white, dear,
> And her hair was so charmingly curled.
>
> But I lost my dear little doll, dear,
> As I played on the heath one day.
> Though I cried for her more than a week, dear,
> I never could find where she lay.
>
> I found my poor little doll, dear,
> As I played on the heath one day,
> Folks say she is terribly changed, dear,
> For her paint is all washed away.
>
> And her arm trodden off by the cows, dear,
> And her hair not the least bit curled.
> Yet for old time's sake, she is still, dear,
> The prettiest doll in the world!

Some girls still had wax dolls, but these were not popular as they were not made to withstand the rigours of everyday wear and tear, and the faces soon became mere blobs of wax. The most common type of doll was one with a fine china face and a stuffed body; if you were lucky, the eyes closed. Later on , it was the "done thing" to have a doll with real hair.

Our group, I won't use the word "gang", was not very doll-minded. We preferred to do something more active than sitting around playing with dolls, and it always seemed to me a waste of time pushing a doll's pram along. However, we nearly all had doll's prams, not the elaborate ones children have today but throwouts from the bigger houses, bought at jumble sales for a few pence.

Doll's houses were few and far between; I cannot think of anyone in our group who had one. I know we had a craze at one time for making doll's house furniture from corks, pins and tiny beads, but I think the "house" for which the furniture was intended consisted of cardboard shoe boxes.

We used to play a variety of card games, usually at Christmas parties. There were "Snap" cards, "Happy Families" and, our favourite, "Animal Grab". The Collinses had a set of "Animal

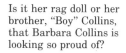
Is it her rag doll or her brother, "Boy" Collins, that Barbara Collins is looking so proud of?

Grab" cards which was used at Christmas—and it was the highlight of their parties.

Most children had crayons, paints, or coloured pencils, and some had colouring books. Jigsaw puzzles were not very popular.

My most prized possession was a mechanical beetle which when wound up would progress slowly across the table flapping its wings. Like so many of our toys it was second-hand; I have an idea it came with several other toys and books from Toby Charters. It gave hours of pleasure and was still going strong in the 1930s. I wonder what happened to it?

I also had a metal swan, greyish green with a red beak and feet and evil black eyes. It was really not designed for water and I think the winder must have rusted as a result of the swan being introduced to its natural element, but the toy was never thrown out; it just disappeared.

The long winter evenings were the time for hobbies, card games and so on. In our house we read from the time the post office closed until it was time for bed. Sometimes, but not often, we did a puzzle, or sorted out our collections of stamps or cigarette cards; now and again we did a few rows of knitting; but reading, by the light of a small oil lamp with one chimney, was our main occupation. There was dead silence in our house for hours every evening; perhaps that is why television seems to me rather a waste of time.

I was a compulsive reader, and still am. The main problem was getting enough books. Not many children had more than half a

The Hopleys, which was occupied by the Tollemaches whose library was "like an oasis in the desert".

dozen books, and those were lent and very often lost. There were books at school, of course, a tattered dirty selection on the bottom shelf of the "silent reader" cupboard; some had been bought with the money allowed for reading books by the education office, some were given by the "gentry" whose children had outgrown them, and some were given when families left the village.

I could never get enough to read, although from a very early age, before I was five, I always asked for books for Christmas and birthday presents. Those that I received in this way were usually of a goody-goody type with death bed scenes, repentant sinners and so on. Most of our birthday books were bought from a travelling salesman who came round about once a month. How eagerly I looked for the visit of the "colporteur"—and how lost I was if he was late. We had one magazine a month from him, *The Children's Friend,* and that had a serial story "The Runaway Princess"—each instalment ended at a crucial point, and we had to wait a whole month before knowing what happened. My aunt took *The Church Evangelist* and, believe me, I even read that from cover to cover.

My maternal grandmother was bed-ridden with rheumatism and did not come downstairs for many years. So it was my job, every Friday after tea, to go upstairs with the two local papers and read her the "Hatches, Matches and Dispatches". There was no heating, of course, and the only light was from a flickering candle. I had to read all the "In memoriam" verses, too.

I must have been a pest to the Collinses, the Aveys, the Borehams and the rest, because as soon as I knew anyone had received a new book for a present I was on the doorstep, begging to be allowed to borrow it. As a great favour, I was allowed to go into the library at the Men's Club now and again and borrow a book from the shelves. Thus I read all the works of Charles Dickens, Walter Scott and Thackeray and a miscellaneous collection of minor writers; anything and everything that came to hand.

Sometimes the Bristols and the Bevans lent us books, and the Tollemaches were very good to us. The thrill of going up to their schoolroom and seeing the shelves full of books, brightly bound and new looking, was to me like finding an oasis in the desert. They had all the G.A. Henty books.

I think the fact that today I am always asking for book tokens as presents, in spite of the fact that there is a library in Bury which I visit at least twice a week, and a fortnightly visit from the mobile library, stems from the fear of having nothing to read!

We were great collectors, too, chiefly of cigarette cards. Maisie Talbot and I had the largest collections in Horringer; the sets we collected then would have fetched a lot of money today if they had

The *Beehive* public house has not changed very much, but the amount of traffic has. The car appears to be the same one seen on page 90; perhaps it was the photographer's.

survived. One of my happiest moments came on a dull February afternoon when I was about nine; I came home from school through a cold drizzle to find that a letter had come for me by the afternoon post (what riches—a second post in those days!) from cousin Marjorie, also an avid cigarette card collector. She had sent me some "swops"—and among those cards was one I had wanted for a long time and had almost given up hope of ever getting, No 32 in *Gems of Belgian Architecture*. I cannot remember now what was shown on that card; all I know is that I had got the set! I felt like the woman in the Bible who had found her lost coin.

Some children collected stamps; Maisie still does. It was far more difficult to collect foreign stamps in those days than it is today. Some boys collected birds' eggs, some collected postcards, some collected marbles; later we collected soldiers' buttons. Soldiers marching through the village were harassed every inch of the way by us children with insistent demands of "Button, button, give us a button!" Not that we got many that way; we had to rely on relations in the forces coming on leave with, we hoped, pockets full of spare buttons! Now and again someone would be lucky enough to acquire a cap badge. That was a red letter day indeed!

The adults of the village also enjoyed their fun and games, or at least the men did. Many of them spent their evenings at the club or in the pubs. Women who did venture into the *Beehive* (never in the *Bells*) were frowned upon by the rest of the female population; normally the women were too tired after their day's work to want to go out in the evenings, even if there had been anywhere for them to go.

The Men's Club was considered the centre of village life, and more respectable than the *Bells* or the *Beehive*. There they enjoyed good fires; several newspapers and magazines sent over from Ickworth when the Family and staff had finished with them; plenty of beer and good company. Many of the men played cards, chiefly crib or whist, and there was a billiard table and a dartboard. Occasionally someone came to give a lecture, usually on politics—everyone was a Conservative, so it was like preaching to the converted—or on world affairs. Now and again a lantern lecture was given or a smoking concert was held.

The only time women were admitted to the club was when an "open" whist drive was held, and then the place was packed to the doors. Of course, we were much too young to go, but we used to see all the prizes; and we would long to possess one of the score cards, which were rather like dance programmes, each card having a tiny pencil attached to it, pink for the ladies and blue for gentlemen.

There was a lending library attached to the club, which was added to from time to time either by the purchase of a few volumes or by gifts of books from the "gentry". At one time parcels of books were sent from Mudies, or books were exchanged with other clubs, but I do not think that can have been very satisfactory for the idea died out with the war.

Cricket was popular with the men, probably because many of them had watched and, on rare occasions, played in the matches arranged between teams from the big country houses. The Hervey men had played cricket for years. In fact, the present cricket pitch had been laid down and maintained by workers on the estate, and the same thing happened at Elveden, Euston and Rougham to name a few. Prince Duleep Singh, the sporting Indian prince who owned Elveden Hall, once organised a team to play at Ickworth.

The village team, run by the Institute, had no proper ground of their own but played on Sam Cooke's meadow, or sometimes Byford's meadow, and they must have eyed the beautiful pitch in the park with envy. That pitch was used less and less by the Hervey family, and on one or two occasions the village team, which consisted largely of the sons of the heads of departments from Ickworth—the estate agent's son, the head gardener's son, John Willie's three sons, Sam Cooke's son, several farmers' sons and sometimes one or two of the footmen at Ickworth were in it—asked for permission to use it. By 1893 the Family had no team at all and the third marquis handed the ground over to the village team though he continued to have it maintained by estate workmen.

The 1914-18 war took its toll and the team went into retirement until it was revived about 1920; apart from the five years of the Second World War it has been going strong ever since. Horringer always had good cricketers; their team in 1922 included Oliver Coster, the son of the head gardener, who could usually be relied on for fifty or more runs each innings; the two Sturgeons of Sharpe's Farm; Mr Catchpole, who lived at Horringer Mill and farmed Street Farm; Tom Last, who was carpenter at Ickworth before the war; Ken Cooke, son of Sam; Jack Honeyball, who was a good all-rounder; Sam Herod, son of the head keeper; the two Smiths from Martin's Green; Sid Curtis, John Willie's son; and Harry Kemish, a footman at Ickworth.

We did not know much about football until 1924 when we became very enthusiastic, as Horringer won the "shield"; what

The Horringer Football Club in the 1922-23 season. Standing, left to right: H. Noyes, C. Leech (the author's father), B. Last, C. Quantrill, T. Last, A. Frost, B. Barkham, G. O. Smith. Kneeling: B. Sturgeon, L. Inglis, W. Avis, J. Honeyball, B. Smith. Sitting: E. Johnson, T. Canham, B. Gotts, D. Boreham and T. Bullass.

shield it was I can't remember—I think it was the Bury and District Village Shield. To add to our enjoyment we beat our arch enemies, Chevington, in the final. As far as I can remember there were two or three replays before the issue was decided, and with each game the rivalry increased. Everyone who could crawl there went to every match.

One enterprising man by the name of "Porky" Nunn ran a van to take supporters to these matches. He was from Chedburgh, so was a "neutral", so to speak. His van, which normally carried pigs—hence his nickname—held twenty people at a pinch, but he must have crammed in seventy or more each time. Luckily we did not have far to go, but how that rickety old van negotiated Weathercock Hill and Queen Hill I don't know. Anyway, he got us there, and got us home.

One other game was played in the village before the war, and that was quoits. There were two "beds" in Horringer, one belonging to the Men's Club and the other to the *Six Bells*. We were more interested in the former as it was situated on the narrow strip of land beyond and opposite the back door of the club on land adjoining the Post Office orchard, so we had a grandstand view of the matches as we sat on the wall of one of my father's pigsties.

Quoits was no game for weaklings. Two iron pegs were driven into the "ground", usually a clay bed, eighteen yards apart, each peg being in the centre of a circle three feet in diameter. Each player pitched two seven-pound iron rings or quoits at the peg in the bed at the opposite end to where he was standing. A "ringer" was a quoit which went right over the peg and scored two points, and a "leaner" was a quoit which did not go cleanly over the peg but leant against it, scoring one point. A score of eleven points was needed when two players were playing, but fifteen was needed when four players were engaged.

Great care was taken of the "beds", which were kept well watered and were covered with sacks when not in use. Each spring the clay was renewed and the bed made up again.

There is a great art in throwing a quoit. Several factors have to be taken into consideration, the most important of which is the force and direction of the wind. Anything that disturbed the concentration of the thrower—a sudden noise or movement among the spectators such as one of us falling backwards off the wall and landing in the pig's trough—would be enough to affect the outcome of a game, so we sat as quiet as mice for hours on end, watching those heavy iron rings being thrown to within a fraction of an inch of the centre peg.

The game was revived after the 1914-18 war, but only fitfully, and it died out altogether before 1939.

REMEMBER THESE
WHO WENT FROM
HORRINGER AND
ICKWORTH TO THE
GREAT WAR AND
DIED FOR KING AND
COUNTRY 1914 1919

Garwood K Alston	Edward W Crick
George W Bailey	Ernest Edwards
Clement B Bevan	George W Finch
Arthur W Boreham	Frank D Finch
Walter Boreham	Walter Gooch
Edmund F Bowers	Charles G Kitcatt
Cecil C Brookes	Edward Last
Samuel Branger	Herbert Last
Frederick C Buckle	Frederick H Paske
Reuben A Burgess	Walter H Peake
Walter W Coman	William C Robbins
Edward J Crack	John T Rowe
Lionel T Crick	William C Sansom
Oliver E Crack	Ernest Sargeant

THE SOULS OF THE
RIGHTEOUS ARE IN
THE HAND OF GOD

CHAPTER TEN

The Great War

WHEN WAR was declared on Germany and Austria on 4th August, 1914, we were really too young to understand what it was all about; I had just passed my seventh birthday. There was no radio in those days and it was the Post Office telephone that brought us the news that war had broken out, so my mother told me to go up and tell Mrs Collins that war had been declared; I went up and told her that Austria had declared war on Hungary, not even realising that those two countries were then part of the same Austro-Hungarian empire.

The outbreak of war more or less coincided with the beginning of the Summer holidays and we were all very excited when soldiers, horses, guns and so on arrived in the village. As usual, we children were in the thick of it as the camp was in the meadow behind the Institute; how very excited we were to see tents going up there. The Institute was taken over by the Army and sentries were posted at the gates.

As well as having to deal with all the extra post office work this entailed, we had two soldiers billeted with us. We girls nearly burst with pride when telegrams arrived for the C.O. and, my father being out on his round or delivering telegrams elsewhere, we were given the job of taking the telegrams to the Institute, answering the question "Who goes there?" with a nonchalant "Friend" and hearing the reply "Pass, Friend" from a grinning six-foot-four guardsman. The big boys nearly died of envy and jealousy to see us pass through the gate.

Our excitement did not last long. We were packed off to stay with friends in Bury until things calmed down a bit, and when we returned home after a week or so the army had gone. Apparently there was not enough water in Horringer for the horses.

After that it was just a case of hearing "So-and-So has joined up"; and a little later, "So-and-So has been killed". As the news of the deaths came by telegram, we very often knew before the relatives did.

My father was crazy to join up. He was thirty-four in 1914. He and his bosom friend, Billy Rowles, went to the recruiting office in Bury together, but it was a case of "One shall be taken, the other

The 1914–18 war memorial in Horringer Church.

Left: Men of the Suffolk Regiment, typical of those who left their villages to go to war.

Opposite: Damage caused in Bury St Edmunds by Zeppelin bombs.

left". My father was the one that was left. He was very short-sighted. He was full of despair. In vain it was pointed out to him that he was of more use in Horringer, where he had a wife and two small children, about four hundred fowls, a dozen pigs and some Belgian hares, as well as the Post Office, a huge garden, an orchard and an allotment; he was like the man in the Bible who would not be comforted. Added to all those responsibilities, his mother, in her sixties, had removed to Bury on her retirement, his mother-in-law in her eighties was bed-ridden in the house next to the Post Office, and two of his sisters-in-law lived there, one completely crippled from polio and the other with a bad heart.

My father was denied the chance to go off to the war, but one night in April, 1915, the war came to us, or at least to Bury St Edmunds, when a zeppelin dropped bombs on the Butter Market and in Chalk Road, killing nine people, I believe. No sooner had the zeppelin departed than my father was off to Bury to see what had happened there, saying that he wanted to make sure his mother was all right. Very laudable, but we knew that he really wanted to see all that there was to see. He called for his friend Dennis Marriott and off they went together on their bicycles— and they were gone for hours, so long that we began to worry about them. However, they came home about six in the morning, full of horrific stories of the scenes in Bury, of wrecked buildings and death and destruction.

This incident made him more than ever determined to join up, and in 1916 he was accepted for a labour battalion. After a short

period in camp at Pease Cottage in Sussex he was sent overseas to Salonika, and that was the last we saw of him till autumn, 1919. He sold up all his animals before he left.

We became quite used to air raid alarms. The best warning we had was from the pheasants who heard the vibrations from bombs and zeppelins before we did. Whenever the pheasants started calling we would get up and crouch downstairs until they became quiet again, when we returned to bed. More bombs were dropped on Bury in April, 1916, and more casualties were caused. We saw zeppelins twice later on, thin silver cigars in the moonlight.

More and more men went away, and more and more "Killed in action" telegrams came. We were not too hard hit by rationing as we were almost self-supporting. John Willie taught us all the patriotic songs, *Keep the home fires burning* and *Tipperary* and the like. Two of his sons were called up. Tom Last won the Military Medal, and there was a lot of talk in the district that Mr Stutters of Chevington had been nominated for the V.C. He did not get it—because he was only a private, people said.

Of the hundred and twenty men who went from Horringer, twenty-six did not return. Rich and poor alike were affected; Clement Bevan of Ickworth Lodge was killed, as was Garwood Alston of Shrublands, as well as his sister's husband; the Cracks lost three sons, the Lasts two. But we were too young to remember them. The military funerals of David Kinsey and William Robbins made a great impression on us, but I am afraid that soon faded with the coming of the "Armistick".

CHAPTER ELEVEN

Grammar School

WHEN I PASSED the "Free Place" examination to the County School in Bury I did not realise what a complete change it would make in my life.

For more than a year I had that exam at the back of my mind, making twice-weekly trips down to Bury after school to be coached by my aristocratic grandmother, who on her retirement as headmistress of some school in Lincolnshire had been found a small house in Horringer Road by my father—not that he got any thanks for his efforts at house-hunting, she contemptuously called it "That hovel". All the same, it was just right for me; I walked down after school, winter and summer, all alone, arriving about five o'clock and, after a quick tea, putting in two hours' solid work before setting off home in the pitch darkness. I rarely met a soul on the way home; there was no one to meet me, for my father was still in Salonika and my mother could not leave the Post Office, as the mail cart did not come until eight o'clock. There were very few houses on the way—after the few around the *Spread Eagle* the next one was West Mill, then the Lodge for Horringer Court, the Red House and the small cottage next door, Great Horringer Hall, the small house on the corner (Cooper's Corner), and then Horringer itself.

I think it was about halfway through the summer term that we had the result of the exam which we had taken in March. I had found the papers fairly easy, though the exam lasted all day, except that I had a qualm about the dictation; I could not for the life of me remember how to spell "opposite"—was it "oppisite" or "opposite"? In the end I made a blot over the "I" or "O".

Anyway, I had passed. I took the letter down to school for John Willie to read. He made no comment until I was putting the Bibles away after Lord Manners' scripture lesson and as I knelt on the floor stuffing the Bibles into the cupboard I heard John Willie say to Lord Manners, "This is the girl who has brought honour to the school!" Then Lord Manners made the remark which became a family saying, "So she should. There's brains in that family. Charles has a fair amount!" The fun we had bringing that saying out when we wanted to tease my father!

Needless to say my aristocratic grandmother was not amused—

a fair amount, indeed! Luckily Lord Manners did not cross her path for years.

John Willie seemed to take all the credit for my success, and he hadn't raised a finger to help as he did not approve of higher education for girls. I was the first girl from Horringer to go to the County School. Two boys were there already, Tom Lloyd, whose

Tom Lloyd, left, and Ken Cooke.

father was Clerk of the Works and who had also won a "Free Place", and Ken Cooke, whose father was a builder and who was a fee payer.

The first question that had to be considered was that of transport. I could not ride a bicycle, so I should have to learn. A second-hand bike was bought for ten shillings from Blake's, the bicycle shop in Guildhall Street, Bury St Edmunds, and I pushed it home. We had several cousins staying at the time, so there was no lack of helpers to teach me to ride. This proved to be a rather painful business, as the first time I wobbled a few yards on my own I ran into the Park gates, though they were open at the time!

The next problem was the fact that I knew nobody at the school; I had never been to Bury alone before, much less on a far-from-safe bicycle. I was promised a new machine when I started school—if I could ride by then. My aristocratic grandmother solved the problem of "knowing other girls" by arranging that I should meet the little girl from the shop at the foot of Horringer Hill, who was starting at the County School the same day as I was. When we did meet Ruby brought her friend Grace, who lived in Westgate Road, Bury, and had won a "Free Place" to the County School; Ruby was going as a fee payer.

When the fateful day arrived I set off just after eight o'clock on my new bicycle, rather excited and very scared, armed with my new satchel, containing pens, pencils and a packed lunch. It had been decided that to begin with Grace, Ruby and I should walk to the school from the *Spread Eagle*, my bicycle being left with my grandmother. Arrived at the school, we were told which form we should be in, 2A being the form for those who had won a "Free Place" and 2B for those who were fee payers; those children who had already been at the school a couple of years would be sorted out according to their academic attainments.

At a quarter to nine a bell rang; we were marched into the main hall; the staff filed on to the platform, one of the mistresses seated herself at the piano, and the headmaster, Mr Judd, announced the hymn *Lord, behold us with Thy blessing*. We should need every blessing there was to spare.

After a few prayers, the door opened and a few children sidled in rather sheepishly and stood by the wall—I thought maybe they were late arrivals, but found out afterwards they were Roman Catholics, who did not come in for the religious part of morning assembly. The staff filed out, the pianist struck up a march, and we all filed out to our classrooms, where we stood at our desks waiting for the arrival of our form master.

Those of us whose first day this was had no idea who would be in charge of our form, but there were sinister whisperings among those in the know, and even the boys looked subdued. Sharp footsteps were heard coming along the corridor, the boy holding the door open straightened himself, we dutifully chorused "Good Morning, sir," and our form master swept in, his black gown billowing behind him. I got the impression of a thin sardonic clean-shaven face, eyebrows meeting over dark impatient eyes, and slicked black hair—not the face of a man who would suffer fools gladly. Such was Mr Felkin, known out of his hearing as "Satan" or "The Devil".

No word of welcome, just a curt "Sit!"—a petrified silence from the class while a boy put out forms for each person to fill in. Full Christian names? surname? date of birth? previous school? father's occupation? reason for coming to this school? and I can't think what else. Text books were given out—"Free Place" children were given theirs free, and filthy they were.

Somehow the day passed, I don't remember how, and then at a quarter past three a bell rang. Time to go home! But no, not for us; only for a few children who had trains to catch. Ten minutes later another bell, and a few more collected their satchels and left. Then at 3.45 our bell. A short prayer, "Lord keep us safe this night", a brusque "Good afternoon" from Mr Felkin, and out we rushed. Well, we didn't dare rush until we were well along the corridor.

I think we were all too tired to talk much, though I had to face an inquisition from my grandmother before I could pick up my bicycle and start the journey home. The weather had changed and it was drizzling with rain. As I pushed my bicycle up Horringer Hill I tried to sort out my impressions, and my overall one was that if this day was typical of those I had to go through for the next five or six years, anyone could have my "Free Place"; give me Horringer School every time.

As I passed the Bench Oak I saw two familiar figures coming to meet me—one of my aunts and my sister. From that moment I began to lead a double life! Answering all their questions with enthusiasm, I praised the school, the other children, and—Heaven forgive me—the staff. I had to paint a rosy picture—everyone would be wanting to hear how I had got on and what it was like, and I knew that any adverse criticism I made would be passed on to the other children by my sister.

The next day, a Wednesday, was not quite so hectic. The

The Bench Oak, a landmark on the road home from Bury.

newcomers were getting used to the wild rush, and also to the change of teachers for various lessons. Maths seemed to occupy a good deal of time, and that meant we saw a lot of "The Devil". I never could decide if he was a good teacher or not; like the rest of the class, I was too petrified to attempt to understand what he was trying to teach us. Later we were to learn that one of his favourite expressions was "You Suffolk nincompoops"; and when he could get no answer to his questions, which he shot at us like bullets from a machine-gun, he would stride up the gangways between the desks knocking all our books on to the floor—bang, bang, bang!

Looking back, I think the man was suffering from shell shock. He certainly shocked us, even those who were good at maths. He usually vented his wrath on the boys—females were not worth wasting his breath on.

Another shock awaited some of us on our third day at the school. On the timetable we had Physical Exercises, or to use the old-fashioned term, drill. We newcomers noted that there was a certain amount of whispering and giggling among those girls who had already had a year at the school, and that they were all wearing a kind of uniform—white blouses and navy blue gym slips. We trooped into the main hall, to be met by an outraged person wearing a gym tunic.

"Where are your tunics?" she demanded of our small group. "Why aren't you wearing them? Didn't you know you wore gym tunics on Tuesdays and Thursdays?"

Someone stammered that no one had told us. At that she gave us her ultimatum, either we turned up on Tuesday properly attired or she would report us to our form master. When we heard that dire threat we agreed that if we could not get tunics by Tuesday we'd all develop pneumonia or something similar and be too ill to come to school.

I was lucky, I had an aunt who made me a tunic out of an old skirt which would serve until we could get to Bury and buy the new material.

No major shocks awaited us on Friday and I cycled home, ready to put the last four days behind me and to pick up where I had left off the previous weekend. I wanted to forget the rush, the strange people, the gym tunics, and "Satan"—especially "Satan"—and to wander in the park discussing our collections of stamps and cigarette cards with Maisie, hearing all about John Willie coping with the fourteen-year-old boys. Above all I wanted to be home.

The next morning I was up bright and early waiting for the gang to appear. At last they arrived and I went out to join them.

"Where are we going today?" I asked.

There was an awkward silence, and then Ivy Boreham said,

"You can't come with us, because you can't belong to our club any more."

I looked at her in amazement. After all, I had founded the club. "Why not?" I asked.

"Well, you made the rule yourself," said Ivy. "You said only children who went to Horringer School should join the club—and you don't go to Horringer School any more—come on, the rest of you!"

Barbara, seeing that for once I was speechless, added, "She's

Zoë Leech with her sister Molly and Ivy Boreham.

right, you know—you said we weren't to break that rule for anybody."

I remembered now. One or two visitors to the village had asked to join and we had been adamant that they weren't eligible to join—and now I was hoist with my own petard. I wished I hadn't been so vehement about sticking to the rules.

They went off down the park, and I wandered down the orchard and sat down under the walnut tree, and thought. As far as I could see, winning this "Free Place" was a dead loss; I had lost a lot and gained very little—I was neither one thing nor another. All I was sure about was that my loyalties would always lie with Horringer, even if I wasn't wanted.

But it hurt. The fall was too big and too sudden. From being a leading light in our village activities, I was nothing; and I certainly would never be a leading light in the County School activities—nor would I want to be.

I wanted to hear about the walk, but I wasn't going to ask. My Christian spirit, never very strong at the best of times, was at a very low ebb. I hoped Ivy would step in a wasps' nest, and that some of the others would fall into that smelly pond by the path to the stables; but they all returned safely.

I thought I would be glad when Monday morning came, but I

was not. The road seemed rougher, and Horringer seemed to be pulling me back; it seemed a quiet warm place without the noise and jostling and indifference of the County School. In short, I was homesick. This seems a ridiculous thing to say, but it was true; and this wanting to go home stayed with me—and is still with me. I am sure I could have done much better at that school if I had not been obsessed with the idea of getting back to Horringer as soon as possible.

I never wasted a moment after school. I rushed round to the bicycle shed, and was always chafing to be gone when Grace and Ruby arrived. They grumbled at my haste but I made the excuse that I liked to get my homework done as soon as possible so that I could have the evening free. Although it was uphill all the way home, the journey seemed easier than in the morning. Talk about "creeping like snail unwillingly to school!" I was a good example of that.

As we became more proficient at cycling in the town we began cycling all the way to school, and that meant we could have a midday break away from school. I used to go to my aristocratic grandmother's to eat my packed lunch, but it seemed a waste of time for me to spend a good hour and a half at hers; the idea began to form in my mind that if I hurried I could get home to Horringer and back between noon and two o'clock. I put this proposal to my mother but she was dead against it, pointing out that it would be far too much of a rush for me, and that my A.G. would not approve. In vain I begged and prayed, my mother was adamant.

The next morning my mother handed me my lunch box as usual. I threw it as far as I could over the wall into the garden, and off I went. When the bell went for the end of the morning session I was off before you could say "Jack Robinson". By the time I reached Byford's corner (the present garage corner) I was beginning to feel rather uneasy.

"I expected you," said my mother as soon as I appeared at the door. "You dropped your lunch box on your way to school this morning. It's on the table—you can eat your sandwiches on your way back to school." And she added menacingly, "Don't you ever do anything like this again, or I'll ask if you can be kept at school during your lunch hour—and not even go down to your grand-mother's."

With that horrific threat, she closed the door behind me. I never tried to go home at lunchtime again.

The weather became worse, it was dark before the end of the afternoon session. A spate of letters from parents came in asking if their children could leave the school early in order to get home before dark. The form teachers were told to discuss each letter and to use their discretion whether or not they allowed the pupil concerned to go early. Needless to say I was in the queue asking for permission to go early. I thought I'd be allowed to go until I saw "Satan's" cold eyes fixed on me.

"Horringer?" he said. "Surely you are not the only one going up that road. There are some boys who go that way—tell them to let you go home with them."

My heart sank. I could imagine what reception I should get if I asked Tom Lloyd or Ken Cooke if I could go home with them. Not on your life! They would never hear the last of it from the other boys. So I went home alone, in the dark.

Whether other parents complained to the Education Office I don't know, but after Christmas the time of the sessions was changed, a quarter of an hour being cut off the two hours we had for lunch and the afternoon session finishing a quarter of an hour early.

The end of term exams didn't worry me unduly—I didn't waste time revising geometry and algebra but concentrated on the subjects I could understand. The one thing that did worry me was the Christmas party, which was held in the evening; either I should be late home or I should have to stay the night in the town. I chose not to go to the party.

My A.G. was horrified—miss a Christmas party! In heaven's name, why? Grace and Ruby offered me hospitality for the night, and my A.G. would willingly have offered to stay up to all hours if necessary. I was worn down by their arguments and reluctantly accepted Ruby's invitation to stay with her. We were due to break up the next day, otherwise I am sure I should never have agreed to spend a night away from Horringer.

On that last day of term a notice was given out by the needlework mistress: "Will those people who have not yet collected their finished garments, please do so before they go home."

After bellowing "Lord dismiss us with thy blessing" with tremendous enthusiasm and grabbing our satchels and various odds and ends, we rushed out to the cycle shed.

"Don't forget your needlework," said Grace.

"Hold my bike," I said to her, and dashed into the needlework room with a hasty knock on the door. I halted in my tracks. Sitting on the cutting out table, holding hands, were "The Devil" and the needlework mistress!

"I've come for my needlework, I did knock!" I blurted out.

"In the basket," gasped the mistress. I grabbed the garment and didn't wait upon my going.

"You weren't long. What on earth's the matter?" said the patient Grace as I ran into the cycle shed.

"The Devil and Miss—, holding hands!" I gasped. Grace, always

111

down to earth, said, "Your imagination! Whoever would want to hold hands with him?" "She seemed to like it," I said—and Grace snorted. (Incidentally, they did get married later.)

It may have been my imagination, but I was not the butt of "Satan's" sarcasm again!

The Christmas holidays passed all too quickly and the first day of term was soon upon us. It was impossible to cycle to school because of the amounts of snow on the roads, so the only thing to do was to walk. Disliking the school as much as I did, I was tempted to stay at home, but I was afraid of missing the notices given out on the first day; once missed, it was difficult to catch up.

A lot of children were away, some because of the weather and others because of the usual crop of winter coughs and colds. Some of the staff were affected, too. I remember one perky boy coming into the classroom between lessons and declaring "Miss Keating was singing a sweet cadenza, when the door opened, and influenza!"

I found I was finding my feet. I no longer crept round the corridors like a frightened mouse. Apart from algebra and geometry I could more than hold my own with the rest of the form and the immaculately dressed children of businessmen, who were inclined to try to lord it over us country children, were sometimes glad to copy my English and History in return for helping me with my maths.

One bright spot—plodding home through the snow, I was given a lift in in the huge dark-green Rolls-Royce with the gleaming brass-rimmed headlights belonging to Mr Charters, of Horringer Manor. No being dropped by the roadside either, he drove right up to my gate. Unfortunately I don't think anyone saw me disembark, as Horringer School had closed early and the children had gone home. I could rely on my sister to broadcast the news to the rest of the school, however.

The snow eventually disappeared, so out came my bicycle again and the lonely rides began. I hated those morning journeys, until one morning as I reached the maple tree Lady Phyllis caught me up, and we went along together. She was doing a nursing course at the hospital, and her hours were more or less like my school hours. The journey did not seem long any more—we could both talk!

Maisie Talbot took the "Free Place" exam that spring and I had hopes that she would pass and be company for me from the next September. Unfortunately Maisie did not pass, which was a great blow to me and, of course, to Maisie herself.

There seemed to be a growing interest among parents in the village in getting their children to school in Bury. Within five years of my first wending my lonely way to the County School, at least twenty children were cycling to school in Bury. Most of them went to the Feoffment School, which was not a grammar school but an ordinary school whose pupils left at fourteen, but at least the parents and children could say they went to Bury school. I don't think Mr Curtis was in favour of such a mass exodus, because he was left with the less bright children.

Time was slipping away and exams were upon us once more, the last before moving up to a higher form. Unfortunately, "Satan" would be moving up as well. As the new form was large it was to be split into two parts, and I was pretty sure that if "Satan" had any choice he would want the part with the brightest maths brains in it, and that certainly wouldn't include me. So I cycled home quite cheerfully on the last day of term and, as I put my bicycle away, my mother met me.

"I've got some good news for you," she said.

Hope springing eternal, I thought perhaps a bomb had fallen on the school as I cycled home, and, if there had to be casualties— well, perhaps "Satan" would be injured just enough to make him give up teaching, or at any rate, teaching at the County School.

"You'll be having company to school next term—Maisie is going in September," my mother went on.

"But what happened? Did she pass then?"

"No," said my mother. "Her aunts are sending her as a fee payer."

Suddenly I realised that the sun was shining!

What happened

Grace—still with us, and living in Westgate Road.

Ruby—still with us, and living in St Leonard's Park. She formerly lived in the house Alpha-Omega, between West Mill and the Horringer Court Estate. Named the house because she said it was the beginning of Horringer and the end of Bury.

Ivy—died from tuberculosis at the age of seventeen in 1923.

Lady Phyllis—still with us and living at Barrow.

The fee payers in our form—all dead.

Mary Armstrong—always reminded me of "the nutbrown maid" with her dark brown curly hair in plaits, her brown merry eyes and her rosy cheeks. Very quiet, she never saw bad in anyone—not even "Satan". When she left school, she went to Norwich Teachers' Training College, and later became head of a small village school near Norwich. The school was near a detention centre for boys, and Mary used to encourage the boys to visit her, and she tried to reform them. She tried once too often, for in 1980 one of them brutally murdered her.

CHAPTER TWELVE

The Newcomers

I CANNOT THINK of a better way to begin this last chapter than with two misquotations, both from the same poem. The first is "Nearly all are gone, the old familiar faces," and the second "All, all, have changed, the old familiar places."

How very true! Horringer has changed more in the last twenty-five years than it did in the previous five hundred. Up to the mid-fifties there had been a trickle of building; from then onwards the trickle became a flood, and the original inhabitants are now a small beleaguered group refusing to be swallowed up by the huge tide of newcomers.

The large development of St Leonard's Park and the two smaller developments of Sharpe's Green and Glebe Close have been built since 1960, and council houses have been built at intervals since 1956. The first group, College Close, consisted of ten houses and seven bungalows, and later four more bungalows were added. Three cottages, Lucas Cottages, were built in 1961, and two more groups, Godfrey's Cottages (six bungalows) and Godfrey's Close (twelve bungalows and maisonettes) were built in 1964 and 1974 respectively. Somehow these council houses have merged into the village well, as for the most part they are tenanted by Horringer-born people.

Most of the other cottages down the village street, originally built in pairs, have been made into single dwellings since being sold by the Marquis of Bristol to those who could afford the price, not Horringer people. One or two larger houses have been built such as The Knoll, The Firs, The Pines and Gravelbury House.

The green has also been affected. The first Rectory in Horringer, which was until 1973 the Men's Club and Institute, has reverted to the status of a private house; the Post Office block is almost unchanged outwardly, though completely modernised inside, part of the building now being called "King William Cottage", I suppose because that part was a public house for ten years; its real name is The Old House.

Opposite the Post Office is Cedar Cottage, which was rebuilt about 1850 for the house steward at Ickworth. Considered a miracle of modernisation when it was rebuilt, it looks very much

The main road today, with Horringer Church in the background.

as it did in 1850 apart from having had water, electricity and central heating installed.

If ever a pretty village has been spoilt by the planners, Horringer has. The thirteenth-century Gildhall, which could have been modernised and still remain beautiful, has been utterly spoiled by being divided into three parts, two fairly large houses with a smaller one squashed in between; the old windows have been replaced by windows with larger panes.

The planners really surpassed themselves here by allowing a double garage to be built right in front of the Gildhall Cottages, effectively blocking the view across the green from the windows of the two cottages at the southern end of the block.

Another sad sight is that of the two large houses built on the green on the site of the old allotments looking across to the church. I will refrain from further comment.

The church is unchanged, though it reached an end of an era with the death of Lord Manners Hervey in 1944. He had been rector for forty-four years.

Tucked away in a corner of the green is the new Community

The thirteenth-century Gildhall before it was altered.

Centre, opened in 1973. The Men's Club have their clubrooms, bar, and storeroom under the same roof as the Community Centre, but maintain their policy of "No connection with the firm next door".

The school house has been turned into two flats, and two groups of cottages were demolished in the early 1960s. These were the hideous, insanitary Flint Cottages, right in front of the Gildhall, and four small cottages, St Leonard's Cottages, built between Mansard Roof Cottage and Cook's Forge.

In the old days, Westley Lane was a quiet country lane, but not any more. Widened in the 1960s, it now acts as a race track for juggernauts and other heavy traffic; as there is no footpath, Heaven help the pedestrian who is intrepid enough to venture down the lane. To add to the danger, the lane joins the A143—the main Bury-Haverhill road, opposite the garage which was put up just after the First World War; with traffic on the main road, traffic coming out of Westley Lane, and traffic going to the garage, the chaos has to be seen to be believed! Five bungalows have been built at the top end of the lane since the end of the Second World War.

There have been changes in Manor Lane, too. A new house was built there just before 1939, and the two small cottages in the lane have been made into one, the thatch being replaced by tiles.

The Rectory, built about 1870, and in which Lord Manners lived for forty-four years, has been divided into two houses; the garden with its well-kept lawns and the rock garden in which he delighted has vanished under the bricks of St Leonard's Park. A smaller Rectory has been built almost on the doorstep of the old one, and was first occupied in 1970. Two houses have been built on what was the kitchen garden of the old Rectory.

The third lane, Sharpe's Lane, which was once thought to be the least desirable part of Horringer, is perhaps the area which has seen the greatest change in character as well as in houses. The old disreputable Six-Row has gone, replaced by two detached houses, one of which is well known for its lovely garden. The occupant of this house, built about 1946, Mr Pask, is one of the few Horringer-born people still residing in the village. Sharpe's Farm is still in being, Mr Gordon Sturgeon who farms there also being Horringer-born. Shrubland Lodge, a very old farmhouse originally known as Whymarks, has changed tenants several times and is no longer a farm house. The rest of Sharpe's Lane as we knew it has gone, swallowed by the new developments of Sharpe's Green and Glebe Close.

Returning to the main road, the house on the corner is rather spoilt by having the replacement for Jackdaw Hall crammed in behind it—another piece of foolishness on the part of the

117

planners. Westabury was once two cottages and is now one, and the same applies to the cottage at Bilson's Gate.

Horringer House, tucked away from the main road, has remained unchanged. It still retains its air of tranquillity in spite of the heavy traffic thundering along the main road.

It is amazing to think how little of the old Horringer is left to us. There is hardly a property which has not been modernised, hardly a yard of land which has not been built upon; gone are the days when we all knew each other, and everyone knew his neighbour's business. We may have running water, electricity, baths and proper sanitation, but the warmth has gone. Horringer is now a village of commuters, here today and gone tomorrow.

As far as Ickworth is concerned, what is left?

The park in which we spent so much of our free time is still open to the public, though it is now administered by the National Trust, who acquired it in 1956. The paths which led to the dairy, stables and Pleasure Grounds are now unused and overgrown, but a new walk has been opened in the Pleasure Grounds, much appreciated by those who like wandering along woodland ways.

The cricket pitch is still in use, and a new sports pavilion

Opposite: The Horringer Community Centre, opened in 1973, which includes accommodation for the Men's Club.

Right: The village sign with the "ounce" or cheetah from the arms of the Bristol family.

replaces the old acorn shed which served as a changing-room for eighty years. A lease of the land was granted by the National Trust to the cricket and football clubs.

The dairy ceased to operate nearly fifty years ago. No milk was then being supplied to the villagers, only to the people living in the mansion and Ickworth Lodge, so its loss was not felt by the majority of villagers.

Ickworth Lodge, divided into two houses, was let to the two daughters as soon as the fourth marchioness died. There have been various tenants since Lady Marjorie died in 1967 and Lady Phyllis moved to Barrow, and it is now a private nursing home.

The Mansion was divided into two parts when the National Trust took over. The Rotunda with its treasures is open to the public on Tuesdays, Wednesdays, Thursdays, Saturdays and Sundays and Bank Holidays during the summer, and the East Wing is set aside for the use of the head of the Hervey family.

Recently there was talk of Ickworth Church being closed; only two services a year are held there, and there is no money left for maintenance and insurance. However, a temporary reprieve has been granted. Many visitors to the Rotunda visit the church, but owing to persistent vandalism the church is now usually locked; the flags carried by the Suffolk Regiment throughout the Boer War, laid up in the church when the third marquis was Lord Lieutenant of Suffolk, have been removed to the Suffolk Regiment's Museum at Gilbraltar Barracks, Bury. The embroidered Royal Arms, supposed to be one of the finest examples of such work in the country and dating from the time of George I, has also been removed.

The lake is still a great attraction for young anglers, but the kitchen garden is a shadow of its former self, with the greenhouses gone.

The local children do not use the park much, preferring to play football and cricket on the village green in spite of the risk to life and limb posed by the roaring juggernauts on the main road.

There is a lot of talk these days about villages dying unless they are developed. Rubbish!! Horringer would never have died. We had all kinds of organisations in the village before we were "developed", and all were flourishing. The atmosphere was far more friendly, and the whole community was more closely knit. Is it unfair to end with the word "Ichabod"—the glory has departed?

The Cedars on the edge of Horringer Green with the beech tree which used to be such a feature of the village scene.

Old Rhymes and Sayings

MANY of the words, the rhymes and sayings which we took for granted when we were young have now died out, so it seems worth putting a few of them on record. With the advent of radio and then of television, added to the scorn poured on dialect speech, so much of the old language has been lost; for myself I cannot see that the old scorned words are worse than the horrible imported words and expressions so often used by children today.

The rhymes we recited fall into several categories. Some were no more than nonsense rhymes, others were in the form of riddles and games. The following rhyme undoubtedly falls into the first category.

> One fine day in the middle of the night,
> Two dead men got up to fight,
> Two blind men to see fair play,
> Two dead men to shout Hooray!
> Two dead donkeys passing by,
> Gave each man a poke in the eye,
> Knocked them through a nine-inch wall,
> Into a dry ditch and drowned them all.

The next little verse seems just as nonsensical, and if that and the one that follows had any hidden meaning, we were quite unaware of it.

> Tiddly-wink the barber
> Went to shave his father,
> The razor slipped and cut his lip,
> Tiddly-wink the barber.

And another barber who should have been more careful:

> I made you look, I made you stare,
> I made you cut the barber's hair.
> The barber's hair was full of lice,
> I made you cut it over twice.

Equally nonsensical but with a very definite message for those who took a lackadaisical attitude to life was:

> Don't Care was made to care
> Don't Care was hung,
> Don't Care was put in the pot
> And stewed till he was done.

There were rhymes about cats, too:

> Not last night, but the night before
> Two tom cats came knocking at my door.
> I went downstairs to let them in,
> They knocked me down with a rolling pin.

> Big A, little A,
> Bouncing B,
> The cat's in the cupboard
> And he can't see me.

I don't know what they meant, they were just rhymes we used to memorise and recite. There were others, though, with which we used to try to catch the unwary.

> Adam and Eve and Pinch-me
> Went down to the river to bathe.
> Adam and Eve were drowned,
> And who do you think was saved?

Woe betide the child who made the obvious reply; he was pinched—hard!

Equally painful for the child who did not duck quickly enough was:

> See my finger, see my thumb,
> See my fist—and here it come!

That might well be described as an action rhyme. Others were more passive, but still designed to catch out those whose wits were not sharp enough:

> Two little ghostesses
> Sat on two postesses,
> Gnawing their fistesses
> Dirty little beastesses,
> How many S's in that?

There were several versions of this catch, one of which was disguised as a tongue-twister:

> Round the rugged rock
> The ragged rascals ran.
> How many R's in that?

The right answer, of course, is that there is neither an S nor an R in the word "that". A rather similar trap for the unthinking was:

> Do you say the yolk of an egg *is* white,
> or the yolk of an egg *are* white?

That caught a lot of children, who were promptly told "Neither, the yolk of an egg is yellow."

Rather similar was the question:

> How many balls of string would it take to
> reach the moon?

The answer, "One, if it was long enough." And then there were the true rhyming riddles:

> Little Anna Hetticoat
> In a white petticoat,
> The longer she stands,
> The shorter she grows.

The answer to that one was "A candle".
Sometimes these sayings could be used to avoid giving a straight

Small boys grow up—Wake Collins in the orchard.

answer. The inquisitive child who asked your age might well be told "I'm as old as my tongue and a little older than my teeth."

Then there was the disguised rhyming game in which another child was invited to chant "Just like me" after every line. It started out innocently enough, and with just a little luck at the end of six lines the answer would come automatically:

> I went up one pair of stairs,
> (Just like me!)
> I went up two pairs of stairs,
> (Just like me!)
> I opened the door,
> (Just like me!)
> I crossed the room,
> (Just like me!)
> I looked out of the window,
> (Just like me!)
> And saw a monkey
> (Just like . . .!)

123

Some of our rhymes were no more than parodies of the proper nursery rhymes:

> Mary had a little lamb,
> Her father shot it dead,
> And now she takes the lamb to school,
> Between two chunks of bread.

Or this one:

> Mary had a little lamb,
> Its feet were black as soot,
> And into Mary's bread and jam
> Its sooty foot it put.

Even popular hymns and Christmas carols were parodied in this way, often with a mixture of advertising culled from a roadside poster or a magazine or newspaper page:

> Hark! the herald angels sing
> Beecham's Pills are just the thing.
> They are gentle, meek and mild,
> Two for a man and one for a child.
> If you want to go to heaven,
> You must take a dose of seven.
> If you want to go to hell,
> Take the blinking box as well!

Or this one, which is still sometimes sung by choirboys out of church:

> While shepherds washed their socks by night
> All seated round the tub,
> A bar of Sunlight soap came down
> And they began to scrub.

Those are harmless enough, but there were some rhymes which were quite spiteful, in use as well as in content:

> Tell tale tit,
> Your tongue shall be slit,
> Every little dicky bird
> Shall have a little bit.

To which the affronted youngster might have replied:

> Sticks and stones will break my bones,
> But calling names won't hurt me!

To finish with an amusing parody of what was at one time a popular song:

> There is a happy land, far, far away,
> Where they have bread and jam
> Three times a day.
> Oh! how the angels yell
> When they hear the dinner bell!
> There is a happy land, far, far away.

Index

Illustrations in bold type

125